90 Days of Encouragement
Volume 2

These daily devotions are designed to encourage firefighters and first responders to grow in their faith. When life seems to be spiraling out of control, and you don't know where to turn, take comfort in the timeless Word of God.

by

International Members
of
FCFInternational

Scripture taken from the King James Version, New King James Version®. Copyright © 1982 by Thomas Nelson. Used by permission. All rights reserved; from the Holy Bible, NEW INTERNATIONAL VERSION®, NIV® Copyright © 1973, 1978, 1984, 2011 by Biblica, Inc.® Used by permission. All rights reserved worldwide; The Holy Bible, English Standard Version® (ESV®) Copyright © 2001 by Crossway, a publishing ministry of Good News Publishers. All rights reserved. ESV Text Edition: 2011; from the Holy Bible, New Living Translation, copyright ©1996, 2004, 2007, 2013 by Tyndale House Foundation. Used by permission of Tyndale House Publishers, Inc., Carol Stream, Illinois 60188. All rights reserved; from THE MESSAGE. Copyright © by Eugene H. Peterson 1993, 1994, 1995, 1996, 2000, 2001, 2002. Used by permission of Tyndale House Publishers, Inc.; the Holman Christian Standard Bible®, Used by Permission HCSB ©1999,2000,2002,2003,2009 Holman Bible Publishers. Holman Christian Standard Bible®, Holman CSB®, and HCSB® are federally registered trademarks of Holman Bible Publishers; Scripture quotations marked NASB are taken from the New American Standard Bible®, Copyright © 1960, 1962, 1963, 1968, 1971, 1972, 1973, 1975, 1977, 1995 by The Lockman Foundation. Used by permission; and Scripture quotations marked NRSV are taken from the New Revised Standard Version of the Bible, Copyright © 1989, by the Division of Christian Education of the National Council of the Churches of Christ in the United States of America. Used by permission. All rights reserved.

Fellowship of Christian Firefighters International
Preface

The fire service can be a difficult place to serve in for Christian first responders. Daily we are bombarded with images and events that test our faith to the very core. Firefighters can take comfort and gain encouragement from the truth contained within the Bible and from others in the fire service who have walked down similar roads.

Christianity is more than a religious system that first responders must keep to please God. Christianity is a relationship with a creator God who loves us and dispatched His Son Jesus Christ to pay the penalty for the bad things we have done in life (John 3:16). Almost every first responder will admit that they have sinned against God (Romans 3:23). Some will even have knowledge in the fact that there is a penalty for those sins (Romans 6:23). For those first responders who confess their sins and believe on the Lord Jesus Christ as their Savior, they will inherit eternal life (Romans 10:9).

Once we have begun our relationship with God, it is important for us to strengthen and grow that relationship. In the fire service, we are used to training to improve our skills and abilities. We watch videos, take on-line classes, and even travel to be proficient in our roles as first responders. If we are willing to go the extra mile in our roles as firefighters, why do some Christian first responders choose not to grow in their faith? The same technology available for training firefighters is available to learning more about Christ.

The Fellowship of Christian Firefighters International is here to encourage firefighters and first responders in their faith. Our desire is to provide resources that not only help you to grow in your faith but help you to thrive in the Department God has called you to.

Meet the Authors

Keith Helms - Keith Helms is a retired firefighter. He was a member of the Charlotte Fire Department for 29 years. He and his wife, Jane, have three grown children and four grandchildren. Keith believed in Jesus Christ as his savior in January of 1980. Early in his relationship with the Lord, Keith was introduced to the ministry of discipleship. His desire to minister in the fire service continues to be focused on discipling others.

Wayne Detzler - Straight after finishing his ministry training at Wheaton Graduate School Wayne, Margaret, and their infant daughter set off for missionary service. Their first assignment was in Germany, where Wayne learned to preach in the atmosphere of a region-wide awakening. Later their son, Mark, was born in Germany before they left for England. For thirteen years they served churches in England, where Wayne also developed a ministry among British police.

In 1983 Wayne and Margaret returned to the United States, where Wayne combined teaching and pastoral ministries. While living in Meriden, CT Wayne became chaplain of the Meriden Fire Department in 1988. He helped to launch a chapter of FCFI. In 1994 he moved to Charlotte, NC where he became chaplain of the Charlotte Fire Department and an active FCFI member. In 2007 he entered his present assignment as chaplain of the Long Hill Fire Department in Trumbull, CT.

The driving force in Wayne's life is making disciples. He takes Matt. 28:19 as a life ministry. Wherever they live, Wayne seeks for guys to disciple. Whether teaching at a local university or meeting with firefighters, he is always looking for F-A-T fellows. These are people who are Faithful, Available, and Teachable. When Wayne finds them, he meets with them to lead them deeper into the Christian life.

Andy Starnes - Instructor Andrew J. Starnes is a lifelong student of the fire service who has been involved since 1992 (volunteer), before becoming a career firefighter in 1998. He is married to Sarah Starnes, and they have a 7-year-old daughter where they reside in Shelby NC. They worship at Putnam Baptist Church. He is a website contributor on the topics of thermal imaging, fire behavior, leadership, and behavioral health, and faith-based devotions for Fire House Magazine, FDIC, Firefighter Toolbox, Fire Department Concepts, Carolina Fire Rescue Journal, Fellowship of Christian Firefighters, and 247 Commitment.

Andrew is the founder of www.bringingbackbrotherhood.org, a non-profit organization designed to encourage and to provide guidance for firefighters in the area of behavioral health and counseling. Articles for these sites are read in several countries and receive approximately 100,000 views per month.

Andrew also serves as the Deputy Chief for the Kill the Flashover Project. He has been featured on the Firefighter Training Podcast, moderfirebehavior.com, FireHouse Magazine, and has presented his tactical thermal imaging course in 23 states and 2 countries outside of the US.

Dan Clegg – Dan Clegg joined the Indianapolis Fire Department on April 23, 1968. Three years later Dan was led to Christ by another firefighter named Joe. Joe was the type of guy who believed it was essential to share his faith in Christ with others. In 1975 Dan began to feel the call of God on his life. Since that time, Dan has pastored a small Methodist church, as well as becoming a fire chaplain. Dan shares the burden to see other firefighters come to Christ as Joe did, and continues to serve as an International Board member for FCFInternational.

Craig Duck – Craig Duck has served in the fire service almost his entire life. After hanging out with his dad in an Upstate, New York fire department Craig became a volunteer firefighter in 1981. Craig went on to become a firefighter in the Washington, DC Fire Department and retired as a lieutenant after 28 years of service. Craig continues to serve his community as a volunteer firefighter in Boydton, Virginia. He and his wife, Holly, have 4 grown children. After receiving Jesus Christ as his Lord and Savior, Craig has worked hard to glorify God in the fire service. Craig currently serves as your President/Missionary.

One Day at a Time – Day 1

By Wayne Detzler – International Board Member and Fire Chaplain (Retired)

"So don't be anxious about tomorrow. God will take care of your tomorrow too. Live one day at a time."
                              Matthew 6:34 Living Bible

Often we beat ourselves up over past failures. On the other hand, we often stress over the future—crossing bridges before we come to them. The Lord Jesus taught us a valuable secret: "But seek first the kingdom of God and His righteousness, and all these things shall be added to you." (Matthew 6:33 NKJV) Dr. Bob Cook turned it into a tagline when he said every day: "Walk with the King." As we daily live by faith, we can safely live in the moment.

1. How does anxiety hurt your faith?

2. How can you overcome anxiety in your life?

2 In and 2 Out – Day 2

By Craig Duck – President/Missionary

Read Galatians 6:1-10

Encouragement for the day – "Bear ye one another's burdens, and so fulfill the law of Christ."

Galatians 6:2 KJV

2 in and 2 out, is a term we are all familiar with. Whether you like the term or not fire departments are required to have two members working together inside a hazardous environment and two members standing by outside prepared to rescue the members inside if they get into trouble. There is always a lot of talk in the fire service about this rule. Some fire departments contend that they do not have enough personnel on the scene quickly enough to abide by this rule and put a fire out. Those in the fire service on the other side of the argument contend that this rule will save first responders lives. No matter where you stand on the issue, it's a rule where those in the fire service will watch out for the interest of others.

Today's Bible verse encourages first responders to bear one another's burdens. There are a lot of firefighters who bear tremendous amounts of burdens that we are unaware of. Caring for sick family members, trouble within their families, difficulties with their marriages, mounting debt, and concern for the future are just a few of the burdens firefighters bear. Day after day firefighters shoulder these tremendous loads without anyone even noticing. Sometimes, though, these loads become too great, and it begins to affect their performance at the station. If we who claim to be Christians never get to know other firefighters on a personal level, we may never even know what burdens they are bearing day after day. Christian firefighters need to find out what burdens our fellow first responders have and begin to help share the load. Not only will you gain a friend, you will also fulfill the law of Christ.

Lord, help me to find a brother or sister first responder who needs my help today.

Encouraging first responders to keep the faith!!

Notes:

_____
_____
_____
_____
_____

Never Leave a Brother Behind – Day 3

By Keith Helms – Battalion Fire Chief (Retired) Charlotte Fire Department and International Board Member

This motto is ingrained in the hearts of firefighters. It was most vividly displayed in the days following 9/11. Untold numbers of firefighters remained on the scene until the last fallen firefighter was found.

It can also be seen every day on the fire scene. Firefighters backing up their brothers. The nozzleman moves forward with confidence because he knows that he is not alone. "2 in 2 out"... a standard that puts the motto into action. Firefighters can take comfort in knowing that their brothers will never abandon them.

Christian firefighters can take an even greater comfort in the assurance that the Lord Jesus Christ will "Never Leave a Brother Behind". Jesus told His disciples that they could be assured that although He would be leaving, no believer would be left behind. He stated that He would come back and take them to the place that He was preparing for them (John 14:1-3). Paul continued this theme when he described the rapture of believers in 1 Thessalonians 4:13-18. The scriptures give us the certainty that no believer will be abandoned.

Christian firefighters also have the daily assurance that the Lord is with them. Again, we see this certainty affirmed in the Scriptures. Matthew 28:20, John 14:1-31, Hebrews 13:5-6, and Galatians 2:20 teach us that God will never leave us. It is because of this certainty that believers can boldly face any trial or tribulation that this world offers. God has not and will not leave us behind.

1. How do these verses provide comfort as you serve in the fire service?

2. What practical ways can you think of that will help encourage other firefighters in your station with this subject?

3. In what ways has the Lord helped you through difficult situations?

Call to Me – Day 4

Dan Clegg – Indianapolis Fire Department (Retired), Chief Chaplain FCFInternational and International Board Member

"Call to Me, and I will answer you, and show you great and mighty thing, which you do not know."

Jeremiah 33:11

In the first week of February, my wife, Donna and I attended an informational class on diets. I agreed to go through this class with her at the time to support her, not knowing what was to come. First, I was going to have three skin spots removed, all of which would come back as cancer. Three different kinds of cancer, no less. Next, this would require more spots to be removed. Then the blood work come back bad. So, the testing for more cancer began. I thought the worst due to my family history and the hazards of being a Firefighter for 33 years. As it turns out, I do not have any cancer at all. However, it was found to be a nonalcoholic, cirrhosis of the liver, which is controlled by the diet that I had agreed to start with my wife in February. We had no knowledge that this diet would also reduce our Glucose reading by 90%. The both of us were booth on Insulin at the time and we needed to get it under control. Is it any wonder that God said, in Jeremiah 29:11 – 14a;

"That He "knew the thoughts I think toward you, says the Lord, thoughts of peace and not evil, to give you a future and hope. And you will seek Me and find Me when you search for Me with all heart. I will be found by you, says the Lord.

1. Do you know His thoughts for you?

2. Are you seeking Him today?

3. Do you hear Him at the door knocking, Revelation 3:20?

Red Flag Warning – Day 5

By Craig Duck – President/Missionary

Read Matthew 16:1-4

Encouragement for the day – "He answered and said to them, "When it is evening you say, 'It will be fair weather, for the sky is red'; and in the morning, 'It will be foul weather today, for the sky is red and threatening.' Hypocrites! You know how to discern the face of the sky, but you cannot discern the signs of the times."

Matthew 16:2-3 NKJV

A friend of mine came up with an idea for a class that he now teaches all around the country. The name of the class is Red Flag Warnings, and it deals with preventing line of duty deaths at fires. After much research and experience, he discovered that most line of duty deaths are preceded by many red flag warnings that go unheeded. We see these red flags going up all of the time at emergencies, but for the most part, we don't experience the pain and suffering of a loss of one of our own. Eventually, as the red flags pile up the inevitable happens and we are forced to go through the pain. The class is designed for the leaders of the department to heed the warnings and change the course of the fireground to ensure a positive outcome.

The Sadducees and the Pharisees came to Jesus one day and asked that He provide a sign from heaven. The only response from the Son of God was this small section in Matthew chapter 16. We are all familiar with the warning signs of unsettled weather patterns, and yet we refuse to see what is happening all around us on a spiritual level. Jesus promised to come back to earth one day to straighten out all of the sin and evil that we have created. As we look at the world around us, I often wonder if that time is right around the corner. Look at all of the red warning flags you see around us today, and you will come to the conclusion that the return of Christ may be imminent. Rather than becoming discouraged about what is going on, it should rally Christian firefighters to rise to the occasion and finish the mission that Jesus showed us in Matthew 28. Do you have what it takes to obediently follow Christ no matter what the world around us is doing?

Lord give me courage today to follow you today no matter what everybody else is saying and doing.

Encouragement, helping one person at a time!!

Persistent Prayer – Day 6

By Wayne Detzler – International Board Member and Fire Chaplain (Retired)

"Rejoice always, pray without ceasing, give thanks in all circumstances; for this is the will of God in Christ Jesus for you."

I Thessalonians 5:16-18 ESV

The Scripture reminds us in various ways to "pray without ceasing." When revival comes, this practice emerges as a moving force. As people pray they become sensitive to the Holy Spirit. When people pray, they also expect God to work. William Carey--the Father of Modern Missions--coined the phrase: Expect great things from God. Attempt great things for God." This humble Baptist lay pastor went to India, where he impacted the entire sub-continent for the Lord. He planted churches, founded a major university, and stopped human sacrifice. It all started, when he as a young man spent hours praying in the chill of northern England.

1. How often do you pray each week?

Answering the Call Help – Day 7

By Andrew Starnes – Captain Charlotte Fire Department and FCFInternational member.

As we face hard times in life, we must remember to share our pain with others. It is not a sign of weakness, but a sign that we are human. Remember, without others calling for help; the fire service would not need to exist.

"The destruction of the weak is the death of fellowship" Dietrich Bonhoeffer.

With that in mind, begin by calling out to God and our brothers/sisters for help. Brotherhood is lifting one another up just as we lift up others who call for help. Consider this tactical benchmark checklist for our lives:

- **Size-Up:** Pray! Tell God what you are facing and share it with someone you trust. "Pray without Ceasing" 1 Thessalonians 5:17

- **Transfer Command:** On an incident, the higher ranking officer takes command upon arrival. In our lives, we don't have to wait on God's arrival. "He is our ever-present help in trouble." Psalm 46:1. He is always there. Let Him take Command.

- **Follow His IAP:** Immediately Apply Principles- God wants us to do our part; which demonstrates our faith (trust) in Him. Start mitigating the problem by following His plan.

- **Report to Rehab:** As we work on the struggles, we face we will become weary.

This is where we are to radio Command: "God, I am tired and weary" And Jesus replies "Come to Me all you who are weary and heavy-laden and I will give you rest (Matthew 11:28)." Remember as a firefighter, when we arrive at an incident, what do we do? We go to work resolving the problem. Why? Because we have confidence in our training and in knowing that help is on the way.

"Before they call I will answer, while they are yet speaking I will hear" (Isaiah 65:24)

So Pray and remember that our confidence is directly correlative to our dedication to God's word. Our 'training' is our study and application of God's word. Then we are to get to work on the problem knowing that help is on the way.

In closing, hard times will come, but it is how we choose to respond to these moments that will impact our lives and the lives of those around us. Let us practice the principles of God's word as the ultimate training for the problems we will all face. For if we fail to train we are training to fail in the very purpose of our lives: our relationship with Jesus Christ.

Notes:

Hazardous Conditions Warning – Day 8

By Keith Helms – Battalion Fire Chief (Retired) Charlotte Fire Department and International Board Member

Should we be nonsectarians? How about pluralists? Apparently, the Christians at the Church in Galatia believed that the answer was "yes." Paul, however, warned them about the hazardous conditions that they were encountering in his letter to the church. His warning was direct and severe. Anyone promoting a "different gospel" was to be accursed, removed from the fellowship.

I wonder what the response would be if this warning were read at every church in our country next Sunday. I wonder what the response would be if this excerpt from the letter were read at invocations like the FDIC. My guess is that in too many situations, the letter and the speaker would be castigated for being intolerant. Paul assumed that the church's response would be accusatory. He covered this by informing them that his intent was to please God, not man.

That is the foundational issue that each of us has to address. Am I trying to please God or am I centrally trying to please man? Heed the warning.

Galatians 1:6-10

"I am astonished that you are so quickly deserting him who called you in the grace of Christ and are turning to a different gospel— not that there is another one, but there are some who trouble you and want to distort the gospel of Christ. But even if we or an angel from heaven should preach to you a gospel contrary to the one we preached to you, let him be accursed. As we have said before, so now I say again: If anyone is preaching to you a gospel contrary to the one you received, let him be accursed.
For am I now seeking the approval of man, or of God? Or am I trying to please man? If I were still trying to please man, I would not be a servant of Christ."

Notes:
_____
_____
_____
_____
_____
_____
_____

125 Unless Otherwise Ordered – Day 9

By Craig Duck – President/Missionary

Read John 14:15-18

Encouragement for the day – ""If you love Me, keep My commandments."

John 14:15 NKJV

When I worked in the District of Columbia Fire Department, we had two-piece engine companies. On box alarms, the wagon would go to the front of the building, and the pumper would go to the hydrant. The pumper driver would hook up to the hydrant and supply water to the wagon to extinguish the fire. The pumper driver would set the pump at 125 psi unless otherwise ordered and then assist the rest of the crew. This simple little phrase would help drivers to remember the correct pressure that was needed to ensure enough water was supplied to the wagon.

John recounts a simple little phrase that Jesus taught him that has a profound meaning. Jesus said; "If you love Me, keep My commandments." As we go through life others should be able to observe that we indeed are Christians by the way we act. While obedience can be difficult in today's world, and especially in today's fire service, we are still commanded to observe the principles that Jesus taught. Don't worry, Jesus didn't leave us alone in the world to try and figure everything out. We have our Bibles that we can read and study which have recorded all of those commandments for us to learn from. He also left believers with the indwelling Holy Spirit to help guide us along the way.

Lord, thank You for this simple little reminder of how I can show my love and appreciation for what you have done.

Encouragement is the word of the day!!

Notes

_____
_____
_____
_____
_____
_____
_____
_____

The Lord is a Strong Tower Day 10

By Wayne Detzler – International Board Member and Fire Chaplain (Retired)

"He only is my rock and my salvation; He is my defense; I shall not be greatly moved."

Psalm 62:2&6 NKJV

King David loved this description of God. As a young man, David had fought his way across the barren, Judean desert. Scattered across this arid area were rock-built towers, the only defense from marauding hordes. David passed on this truth to his son, Solomon, who wrote: "The name of the LORD is a strong tower; The righteous run to it and are safe." (Proverbs 18:10 NKJV)

1. How can you demonstrate this Biblical principle in your department today?

2. How has God provided you safety during emergencies this past year?

3. How can you praise the Lord in each circumstance?

Saturday Morning Clean-up – Day 11

By Keith Helms – Battalion Fire Chief (Retired) Charlotte Fire Department and International Board Member

Read John 13:1-20

One of the daily duties in the Charlotte Fire Department is the clean-up of the fire house. Today is Saturday, and this is the day of the week that the Charlotte Fire Department designates for an extended clean-up of the fire house. On the other days of the week, a light clean-up is acceptable. But Saturdays are different. The floors are stripped and waxed. Everything is dusted. Refrigerators and ovens are cleaned. Bathrooms are cleaned and sanitized. Clutter is removed from the apparatus area and storage rooms. At most fire houses, the firefighters help each other to make sure that all areas are completed. Then, later in the day, the Battalion Chief will inspect the station (I wasn't very good with that assignment). The inspection insures that the clean-up is thorough and complete. When a station is negligent in the daily and weekly clean-up duties, the effects are readily detected with sight and smell. Most firefighters take pride in a well-kept station.

As believers, we also need daily clean-ups. The problem is that we cannot clean ourselves of the filth of sin

(Jeremiah 2:22). We cannot cleanse ourselves with religious and spiritual performances (Psalm 51:16-17). All that we can do is confess and admit that we need someone else to do the cleaning. And that someone is God alone (1 John 1:9, Psalm 139:23-24). Any cleansing that we do ourselves is similar to a firefighter that I once knew. When he needed a shower after a fire, he would simply use a heavy dose of cologne. You may not readily detect the body odor, but it's still there. God alone can cleanse your heart. Without the working of the Holy Spirit, you may have a lot of spiritual activity, but when the dust settles, the stain is still there.

Sometimes a more extensive cleaning is needed. When a particular sin has become persistent, the believer may need to seek the help of others. There are numerous passages in the scriptures that refer to encouraging and building up of one another. Just like a firefighter may need help to complete his clean-up, God often uses other Christians to walk with us and help us as we are seeking repentance and personal revival. However, it is still God alone that can cleanse.

We should always seek to have a pure heart. It is a reflection of our relationship with the Lord. Ask the Lord to inspect your heart. Acknowledge your need for cleansing. Thank Him and worship for His mercy and grace.

Underlined Bible – Day 12

By Wayne Detzler – International Board Member and Fire Chaplain (Retired)

From Margaret's Underlined Bible

"Who has believed our message? To whom has the LORD revealed his powerful arm? My servant grew up in the LORD's presence like a tender green shoot, like a root in dry ground.

Isaiah 53:1-2 NLT

In our shared study Bible, she underlined these words. They reflect the heart of an evangelist--Margie's overwhelming spiritual gift. As we share the saving news of salvation, many--if not most--reject it. Even in our families, we see this. Still, the loving, nail-pierced hands of Jesus are outstretched. He welcomes all, who come to him by faith.

1. How often do you and your spouse pray together?

2. Who in your family needs prayer for salvation?

Moral Superiority – Day 13

By Keith Helms – Battalion Fire Chief (Retired) Charlotte Fire Department and International Board Member

Read Luke 18:9-14

What standard do you use to measure your level of morality? If you are using the world as your measuring tool, you may proudly determine that you are doing fairly well. Think about this: I am 5'8" in height. If I stand in the midst of a group of very short firefighters, I can be confident that I am an extremely tall person. However, if I walk out onto the court of an NBA game, I quickly realize that I am vertically limited. The same picture applies to our level of spirituality. If other people are my standard, then I can convince myself that I am doing well. However, if Jesus Christ is my standard, then my sinful flesh is exposed. I realize that I am still in the refining process and I need total dependence on the Holy Spirit to daily battle the flesh that still resides in my heart.

God resists those with a proud heart. He blesses those with a humble, broken heart.

Luke 18:9-14

He (Christ) also told this parable to some who trusted in themselves that they were righteous, and treated others with contempt: "Two men went up into the temple to pray, one a Pharisee and the other a tax collector. The Pharisee, standing by himself, prayed thus: 'God, I thank you that I am not like other men, extortioners, unjust, adulterers, or even like this tax collector. I fast twice a week; I give tithes of all that I get.' But the tax collector, standing far off, would not even lift up his eyes to heaven, but beat his breast, saying, 'God, be merciful to me, a sinner!' I tell you, this man went down to his house justified, rather than the other. For everyone who exalts himself will be humbled, but the one who humbles himself will be exalted."

Notes:

_____
_____
_____
_____
_____
_____
_____
_____

Fire Patterns – Day 14

By Craig Duck – President/Missionary

Read I Corinthians 4:14-21

Encouragement for the day – "Therefore I urge you to imitate me."

I Corinthians 4:16 Holman Christian Standard

When I was a fire investigator fire patterns were an important part of the investigation. As we looked at the remains of a fire, we would carefully examine them for any patterns that would give us a clue as to how the fire started. These patterns could help us determine if an accelerant was used, if the fire was caused by an electrical problem, if the area had experienced a flashover, and ultimately where the fire had started. Without these patterns available to the fire investigator, it would be difficult to determine the origin and cause of a fire.

As Christian first responders, we are called to set a Godly example to others in the fire service. Our lives should be a pattern for others to show them how to live a life that is pleasing to God. Paul said "imitate me" in my faith and the effective daily practice of it. The Gospel message is powerful because the Holy Spirit can change lives from sin and darkness into a new creation. This message is not only preached in love through the words we say but more powerfully through our actions. When others look at the pattern we leave behind, what do they see?

Lord, help me like Paul to be a Godly pattern in my department that others want to follow.

Encouraging those around us is a 24/7 responsibility!!

Notes

_____
_____
_____
_____
_____
_____
_____
_____
_____
_____

The Arsonist Within – Day 15

By Wayne Detzler – International Board Member and Fire Chaplain (Retired)

"Take control of what I say, O Lord, and guard my lips.'
                                                    Psalm 141:3 NLT

Each day this prayer is pertinent in my life. The New Testament warns us: "And among all the parts of the body, the tongue is a flame of fire... It can set your whole life on fire, for it is set on fire by hell itself." (James 3:6 NLT) In this dramatic picture, James says our tongue is literally an arsonist. Over 20 years as a fire chaplain I saw the devastating work of arsonists many times, and James reminds me that my speech can have the same effect. So I pray: "Guard my lips! O Lord."

1. In what ways do you use your tongue that is displeasing to God?

2. How can you better avoid using your tongue from evil?

A Lifetime of Learning – Day 16
By Craig Duck – President/Missionary

Read II Peter 3:14-18

Encouragement for the day – " but grow in the grace and knowledge of our Lord and Savior Jesus Christ. To Him be the glory both now and forever. Amen."

II Peter 3:18 KJV

As I was talking to a young firefighter the other day, it dawned on me that I have been around the fire service for over 30 years. During that time I have learned a lot about the art of firefighting. One of my passions over the years has been to learn as much as I can about the various emergencies that we get called out to. I have read books and magazines, attended classes, and talked with manufacturers to gain as much knowledge as possible. We respond to a wide variety of calls, and it is important to know how to mitigate each one in a safe way. There are many first responders who do not feel that learning is important and it shows in their performance. In fact, we in the fire service will typically poke fun at those who never learn.

Christian first responders should desire to know more about God each and every day. There are so many who never grow and learn. Like the rookie that never desires to truly know how to be a good firefighter, some Christian first responders are comfortable in their infant state. God desires for us to grow spiritually. Our earnest desire should be to learn as much about God through reading, studying, and memorizing the Bible. Like desiring water after a big fire to quench our thirst, so should we desire to be in the Word of God each and every day to learn more about the one that loves and cares for us. Spiritual growth should be as natural to the Christian first responder as it is to the firefighter who wants to learn more about the fire service. How about you, do you regularly read and study your Bible?

Lord, thank You for giving us the Bible that we might be able to grow in our knowledge and love for You.

Encouraging first responders to keep the faith!!

Is Your Blesser Broke – Day 17

By Wayne Detzler – International Board Member and Fire Chaplain (Retired)

"But of Him you are in Christ Jesus, who became for us wisdom from God—and righteousness and sanctification and redemption—that, as it is written, 'He who glories, let him glory in the LORD.'"

I Corinthians 1:30-31 NKJV

When Bob Hopkins discipled me, he taught me to memorize this passage. "But of Him, you are in Christ Jesus, who became for us wisdom from God—and righteousness and sanctification and redemption—that, as it is written, 'He who glories, let him glory in the LORD.'" (1 Cor. 1:30-31 NKJV) It embraces the entire work of the Lord in our lives—wisdom to know Him, righteousness to live for Him, sanctification to become like Him, and redemption because we are completely free in Him. Now, if that doesn't bless us---our "blesser" is broke!

Notes:

_____

_____

_____

_____

Heavy Fire Showing – Day 18

By Craig Duck – President/Missionary

Read I Kings 18:20-40

Encouragement for the day – "Then the fire of the Lord fell and consumed the burnt sacrifice, and the wood and the stones and the dust, and it licked up the water that was in the trench."

I Kings 18:38 NKJV

When I worked in the District of Columbia Fire Department, there were several of us who would have a little fun with the term "heavy fire showing." When we would see the officer who made that size up, we would ask him/her if the fire was coming out the windows and falling toward the ground because of its weight. The point was to give an accurate size up, and the term heavy fire was subjective. Some used the term when fire was coming out of more than one window and others only if one or more floors were on fire. I only made a statement like that in my size up when fire was falling to the ground, which it never was.

The Bible talks about a time when fire fell from heaven. Elijah the prophet had a contest between God and Baal to prove that there is only one God and not many.

The prophets of Baal went first and tried everything they could to call down fire from heaven to start a fire for the sacrifice. Nothing they did worked and Elijah even mocked them saying; "Cry aloud, for he is a god: either he is meditating, or he is busy, or he is on a journey, or perhaps he is sleeping" (verse 27). After soaking the wood for the sacrifice, Elijah cried out to God and fire fell from heaven and ignited the wood. Today Christian firefighters see people worshipping all sorts of god's in many different ways. Don't be mistaken the Bible plainly talks about the one true God and His Son Jesus Christ. He desires to have a relationship with you, and the invitation is open to all. Learn how to know for sure that you will go to heaven when you die by visiting our website www.fellowshipofchristianfirefighters.org and go to the "God's plan for Christian firefighters page in the training section.

Lord thank you for your salvation which is so rich and so free.

Encouraging those who have no hope!!

Genuine Joy – Day 19

By Wayne Detzler – International Board Member and Fire Chaplain (Retired)

"the joy of the Lord is your strength."

Nehemiah 8:10 NLT

We called it a "tabernacle." It was a simple board building that stood behind a local funeral home. The seats were benches made out of planks. Scattered on the floor were wood shavings. And the place jumped with joy. Sunday after Sunday hundreds of people crammed into the Tabernacle. The singing was loud; the preaching was powerful. When the Holy Spirit moves, "the joy of the Lord is your strength." (Nehemiah 8:10 NLT) The unlikely instrument of revival in the gritty industrial city of Pontiac, Michigan was an engineer turned preacher. His name was H. H. Savage, and the Holy Spirit anointed him to reach a whole generation of factory workers in suburban Detroit. Joy electrified the atmosphere in the old board building behind Huntoon's Funeral Home. I know because I was there.

Attic Fires – Day 20

By Craig Duck – President/Missionary

Read James 5:13-18

Encouragement for the day – "Confess your trespasses to one another, and pray for one another, that you may be healed. The effective, fervent prayer of a righteous man avails much."

James 5:16 NKJV

   Attic fires can be some of the more difficult fires that we respond to. I have been on many over the years, and each one presents different challenges for those attempting to extinguish the fire. A coordinated attack led by an experienced crew is always the best chance for success. The right amount of water must reach the seat of the fire to knock down the flames. Timely ventilation is also a key element in the operation. Too much ventilation and you will accelerate your chances of a flash over where not enough ventilation or poor ventilation will lead to extreme heat conditions and the inability to reach the seat of the fire. Everyone working together in harmony and with purpose will allow the crews to put the fire out.

   Prayer is a powerful weapon in the hands of a Godly firefighter. Those who choose to use it effectively can truly change the course of their department and those who serve there. James uses a term that is not often used in today's fire service. The idea of a "fervent prayer" is to have a passionate intensity to what you are praying for. Often people treat prayer as if it were a wish list that you give someone at Christmas time. God has designed prayer to be sincere and heartfelt. The idea is to pray for others needs before our own and always so that God will be glorified within each circumstance. Like an attic fire, our prayer time needs to be a coordinated event that has purposeful meaning. Praying regularly, with other Christian firefighters and for specific requests within God's will is a good way to be effective in your prayer life.

Lord, help me to make prayer a priority in my life. Show me the needs of others in my department that I might begin to pray for them.

Encouragement, setting the standard in the fire service!!

Fire Falls – Day 21

By Wayne Detzler – International Board Member and Fire Chaplain (Retired)

When the prophet Elijah challenged the false prophets of Baal, God answered with fire. From heaven, fire fell and consumed the sacrifice Elijah had offered. (1 Kings 18:36-39) Immediately the people cried out: "The Lord--He is God! Yes, the Lord is God!" (1 Kings 18:39 NLT) This is a powerful picture of true revival. When the fire of the Holy Spirit falls, people immediately recognize that God is at work. In Indonesia, during the 1970s the fire of revival fell, and the beleaguered believers were empowered to see mighty miracles and multitudes of conversions. It all starts, when we get a true picture of our great God.

Notes:

_____
_____
_____
_____
_____
_____
_____

Not Qualified – Day 22
By Craig Duck – President/Missionary

Read I Timothy 3:1-7

Encouragement for the day – "Here is a trustworthy saying: Whoever aspires to be an overseer desires a noble task."
I Timothy 3:1 NIV

Have you ever been told that you are not qualified? In the last several years this term has been used for hiring and promotion within the fire service. It is always disappointing when you are trying to obtain a job or a higher position only to hear that you are not qualified. Some promotional systems pick from candidates who are highly qualified and qualified but never from the not qualified group. Firefighters and first responders who are serious about promotion will work hard to ensure that they end up in that highly qualified group.

Paul describes two church offices in I Timothy chapter 3, that of an overseer (pastor) and deacon. The importance of having qualified men who can function in this position is vital. Christian firefighters and first responders should strive to meet these qualifications so when God calls you to serve in this capacity, you won't be disqualified. The local church is important to God and how they should govern themselves is spelled out in the books of first and second Timothy as well as Titus. It is vitally important that those in leadership be ready for the task. We understand the importance of having good leaders in the fire service, and it is no different with God and His church. So take a few minutes to read over the qualifications that Paul presented for overseers in this section of the Bible and work hard to meet them. You never know when God might be calling you to the ministry.

Lord thank you for this little reminder that the standards you set are high, help me today to meet them.

Encouraging firefighters and first responders to keep the faith!!

Notes

_____
_____
_____
_____
_____
_____
_____

The Need to Vent – Day 23

By Andrew Starnes – Captain Charlotte Fire Department and FCFInternational member.

Have you ever felt the pressures of life, the job, and stress mounting up to such a point that you felt you were going to explode?

As firefighter's we know that pressurized cylinders and containers have devices in place to relieve the pressure if it reaches a dangerous level. These PRV's are there to help alleviate the pressure and bring things back to a manageable level.

What about our own personal need to "alleviate pressure and bring things back to a manageable level?"

What happens when we don't alleviate the pressures of life in healthy ways, and we explode on the ones we love?

What happens when we don't alleviate the pressures of life and say things we shouldn't to others in person or on social media?

Is it fair to our loved ones that "our stressors" have now caused collateral damage to their lives?

Let us consider a new relief valve: A prayer relief valve.

"Let go of anger and leave rage behind! Don't get upset—it will only lead to evil"(Psalms 37:8 CEB)

But how do we vent in a healthy way? Where can we go? Who can we talk to?

As firefighters, we do everything together yet we seem to forget that we are not meant to carry these burdens alone.

<u>The Application:</u>

1) There is strength numbers:

From the very beginning, each of us should seek out a group that we may confide in. They should be a frequent number on our call list.

"Two are better than one because they have a good return for their labor. For if either of them falls, the one will lift up his companion." Ecclesiastes 4:9

Let us learn to turn to God and to our group so we can vent in healthy ways instead of blowing up on others.

2) Lift each other up:

"But woe to the one who falls when there is not another to lift him up." (Ecclesiastes 4:9, 10 NASB)

Too often we think that we must provide the answers for the troubles that our friends and loved ones face. This is a great failure on our part.

Our role is to show up, shut up, and lift up. It is God who ultimately provides the answers and healing. It is our role to be the "hands and feet of Christ" which means to physically show up in the lives of those who are hurting around us.

In closing, we all need someone to vent to. It takes a true friend to let us unload our burdens without thinking we are aiming our frustrations at them. It takes a true friend to tell us what we need to hear and not what we want to hear in those moments.

Let's step up and be that friend to a hurting brother or sister today!

You may be the answer to their prayer.

Revival Response – Day 24

By Wayne Detzler – International Board Member and Fire Chaplain (Retired)

When the Holy Spirit falls in power on God's people, there is a harvest of people coming to Christ. At City Church in New Haven, CT people come to Christ on a regular basis. When Steven Furtick launched Elevation Church in Charlotte, NC they were overwhelmed by the harvest of Millennial young adults coming to Christ. A few miles away Derwin Gray saw a similar response at Transformation Church. Revival is harvest time. I have seen it almost everywhere we have served and preached. Jesus said, "Wake up and look around. The fields are already ripe for harvest." (John 4:35 NLT)

1. How has God used you in the past year to share the Gospel message to other firefighters and first responders?

2. Who do you know in your station needs to hear the salvation message?

Acting Officers – Day 25

By Craig Duck – President/Missionary

Read James 4:7-10

Encouragement for the day – "Draw near to God, and He will draw near to you. Cleanse your hands, you sinners; and purify your hearts, you double-minded."

James 4:8 NKJV

    Years ago before I was promoted to the rank of sergeant in the District of Columbia Fire Department, I was called upon to act as one. An acting officer doesn't receive any increase in pay but is required to fulfill all of the duties of an officer. The actor rides the front seat of the apparatus and makes all of the decisions for the company on emergencies. As information is received, it must be prioritized and acted upon to resolve the crisis at hand. During the day as administrative situations would arise, the acting officer must handle them as if he/she were the actual officer. While I spent time waiting to get promoted, I learned a lot about dealing with personalities, handling emergencies and making decisions to better the company I was working with.

    The Bible contains truth that is relevant to today's Christian firefighters. Once the information is received via personal Bible reading, studying or listening to a sermon the hearer then has a choice to make. Will I act upon what is said, or will I continue as before? It is essential for us to act upon the truth of the Bible. We cannot force others to believe; we simply must afford them an opportunity to act upon that truth as well. When a truth is brought home, don't allow it to pass without any change. Confess your sins to God and allow His power to rest upon your life. So often we firefighters attempt to handle every emergency in our lives under our own power and in our own way. God desires for us to draw nearer to Him and follow all of His ways.

Lord, thank You for helping me through tough and difficult times in my life, may my life glorify You today.

Encouragement, the art of lifting people up!!

Notes

_____
_____
_____
_____
_____

God is Still Calling – Day 26

By Wayne Detzler – International Board Member and Fire Chaplain (Retired)

"Then how is it that each of us hears them in our native language? Parthians, Medes and Elamites; residents of Mesopotamia, Judea and Cappadocia, Pontus and Asia," Acts 2:8-9 NIV

The gospel is for all. One of the great joys of evangelism is seeing people of every background and culture come to faith in the Lord Jesus. After the day of Pentecost, Peter summarized in this wonderful passage: "Each of you must repent of your sins and turn to God, and be baptized in the name of Jesus Christ for the forgiveness of your sins. Then you will receive the gift of the Holy Spirit. This promise is to you, and to your children, and even to the Gentiles—all who have been called by the Lord our God." And we are so thankful that God is still calling people to believe in Him.

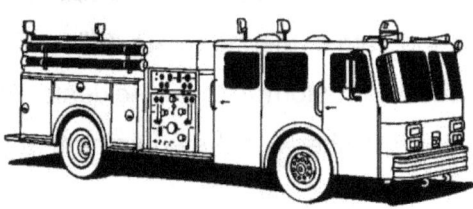

Preparing for the Storm – Day 27
By Craig Duck – President/Missionary

Read Isaiah 25:1-6

Encouragement for the day – "For you have been a stronghold to the poor, a stronghold to the needy in his distress, a shelter from the storm and a shade from the heat; for the breath of the ruthless is like a storm against a wall,"

Isaiah 25:4 ESV

As the east coast braces for hurricane Joaquin, fire departments are getting prepared. Most of the major cities have an emergency operations plan (EOP) that they will follow with specific instructions for fire departments outlined in an incident action plan (IAP). Whether it is up staffing additional units, moving companies that could be in danger of flooding or acquiring additional resources departments are preparing for the worst while hoping for the best. Having gone through several of these storms as a company officer, I am confident that the vast majority of firehouses in the path of the storm are drilling on the proper procedures for storm-related incidents. At the very least firefighters are checking the equipment at the station and ensuring that everything is ready for the impending storm.

God protects His people in all kinds of storms. Just as we can't stop the hurricane from coming, the storms of life will eventually come to every believer. Christ has gained the victory and praises should be continually offered in thanks to Him. Christian firefighters should abide in Christ at all times, especially during the difficult days when ones faith is being tested. God has never failed on any of His promises, and He invites His people to take refuge in Him. While we would love for the storms to go a different direction, God in His infinite grace says "I will be with you through the storm." Trust in God; He will never let you down.

Lord, thank you for always being there for me, even in times of crisis.

Encouraging first responders to keep the faith!!

Notes

_____

_____

_____

Reasoning Together – Day 28

By Wayne Detzler – International Board Member and Fire Chaplain (Retired)

"'Come now, and let us reason together,' Says the LORD, 'Though your sins are like scarlet, they shall be as white as snow; though they are red like crimson, they shall be as wool.'" (Isaiah 1:18 NKJV) Isaiah leads the way to forgiveness, and he shows us the breadth and width of God's great forgiveness. Some people are burdened down, as Isaiah says: "Woe to those who draw iniquity with cords of vanity and sin as if with a cart rope." (Isaiah 5:18 NKJV) The Lord Jesus reminds us that He alone can lift the burden when he says: "Come to Me, all you who labor and are heavy laden, and I will give you rest." (Matthew 11:28 NKJV) The hymn writer helps us sing: "Sovereign grace o'er sin abounding. Ransomed souls the tidings tell." (William Bradbury)

Notes:

_____

_____

_____

_____

_____

The Slack Man – Day 29

By Craig Duck – President/Missionary

Read Colossians 4:7-15

Encouragement for the day – "Greet the brethren who are in Laodicea, and Nymphas and the church that is in his house."

Colossians 4:15 NKJV

During a live fire training exercise that I attended the other day, I learned about the slack man. This particular department taught its members the importance of the third person on the hoseline. While we all want the glory of being on the nozzle, it takes a team of people working together to reach the seat of the fire. The slack man's responsibility is to ensure that the nozzle person never runs out of hose. Rarely recognized for doing his/her job well, this vital position ensures a smooth operation for the hose team. The slack man typically is not where the action is but always allows the rest of the team to reach the action and is a vital position for success.

In a letter to the Colossians Paul gives his final greetings in chapter 4. Within this final greetings section, we learn of a lot of people who helped Paul in the ministry. While many folks over the years have praised Paul for the work he accomplished, he was not alone. Like a hoseline crew, it takes a team of dedicated people to run an effective ministry. While we don't know much about Nymphas, his role must have been crucial for the success of Paul's ministry. In a day and age when everyone desires to be in the spotlight, God is still calling people to silently serve in the background. Perhaps God has been speaking to you through your Bible reading to help out a particular ministry. I would encourage you to answer that call and serve God with everything you have. God truly will be glorified in the fire service when we all do our part.

Lord thank you for this reminder to faithfully serve you no matter how big or how small the task may be.

Encouragement begins with you!!

www.fellowshipofchristianfirefighters.org

Notes

_____

_____

_____

_____

Leading Others – Day 30

By Andrew Starnes – Captain Charlotte Fire Department and FCFInternational member.

How can we lead others if we cannot lead our own hearts?

"Give me wisdom & knowledge that I may lead this people for who is able to govern this great people of yours?"
                                                            2 Chronicles 1:10

How can I lead others O God when I can't even lead my own heart?

How complex is the journey to empowering those who would rather be chained by their behaviors? In our minds, we justify our decisions and surround ourselves with those who agree with us.

Proverbs 3:5 says "Trust in The Lord with all your heart and lean not on your own understanding."

We cannot be wise by our own understanding. We must seek wisdom. There are limits to our knowledge and capabilities but "with God all things are possible."

Great power produces neither peace nor security. Treat it with the caution it deserves & you will guard your heart from destruction. Lead from a pure motive. A motive to share God's love through Jesus. This is wisdom.

Wisdom in knowing that your source is limitless when you submit to His authority. Your understanding will grow as you come to know and understand Him.

When you allow the one who made your heart into your heart, you can touch the hearts of others.

Let Him lead you, and you will be a leader like none other...

Notes
_____
_____
_____
_____
_____
_____
_____

Offended by a Coworker – Day 31

By Keith Helms – Battalion Fire Chief (Retired) Charlotte Fire Department and International Board Member

"Be sober-minded; be watchful. Your adversary the devil prowls around like a roaring lion, seeking someone to devour."

I Peter 5:8 ESV

Have you ever been offended by a coworker? Maybe you were falsely accused of an infraction or slandered in some way. How did you deal with the situation? While there is no step-by-step pattern of how we should react, the Scriptures do give us some guidelines.

In Luke 6:27-36, Christ exhorts us to treat our offenders in the same manner that He did. ""But I say to you who are listening: Love your enemies, do good to those who hate you, bless those who curse you, pray for those who mistreat you. To the person who strikes you on the cheek, offer the other as well, and from the person who takes away your coat, do not withhold your tunic either. Give to everyone who asks you, and do not ask for your possessions back from the person who takes them away. Treat others in the same way that you would want them to treat you."

If you are confident and strong in your relationship with Christ, then you have the capacity to respond to offenses in a way that reflects the image of Christ and in a way that is in opposition to the world and the desires of your flesh. Turning the other cheek tells the offender that he/she is impotent to control your heart and mind. The offense hurts (just as a strike on the cheek), but the pain does not need to determine your thoughts or actions. Let the scriptures and the Holy Spirit direct your path. Also, when offended, make yourself accountable to a Christian brother who is not afraid to tell you when you are responding according to flesh, not the spirit.

For further study, begin with Romans 12:1-21

Notes:

_____
_____
_____
_____
_____
_____
_____

But Thanks To God – Day 32

By Wayne Detzler – International Board Member and Fire Chaplain (Retired)

"But thanks be to God, who gives us the victory through our Lord Jesus Christ."

1 Cor. 15:57 ESV

Paul's paradigm of victory is resurrection. Because the resurrected Christ triumphed over the grave, He shows us the way to ultimate victory in our lives. We know that we will have a new body and a new life, when we share in His resurrection. We will also share in His glory. As the songwriter put it: "O that will be glory for me." As the climax to 1 Corinthians chapter 15, Paul draws this conclusion: So, my dear brothers and sisters, be strong and immovable. Always work enthusiastically for the Lord, for you know that nothing you do for the Lord is ever useless." (1 Cor. 15:58 NLT)

1. When was the last time you thanked God for His wonderful salvation?

2. Are you working enthusiastically for the Kingdom in your department?

Bailout System – Day 33

By Craig Duck – President/Missionary

Read Matthew 11:25-30

Encouragement for the day – "Come unto me, all ye that labour and are heavy laden, and I will give you rest."

Matthew 11:28 KJV

In the last several years' bailout systems have become popular. Several times in my career I have been asked to test out a few of those systems at our training academy. Each one of the systems had its positives and negatives. These systems have been designed to be used to help the firefighter escape from an untenable situation where he/she has no choice but to go out the nearest window. The system that the District of Columbia was working on several years ago was integrated into the firefighting pants and has several features. When a couple of us began wearing the pants a lot of the other firefighters would poke fun at us calling them quitter pants.

Life can be difficult for today's first responder. The stress of our work and the things that we witness can take its toll on us physically, mentally, and even spiritually. Not only can it be difficult serving in our departments, but other stressors such as finances, family, and health can add to our difficulties. Divorce is high among first responders and suicide is on the rise, all pointing to the fact that sometimes we all need some help. We always feel like we are the heroes, but where do heroes go when they are at the end of their rope? Jesus calls quietly to us to come to Him in times of trouble and when the storms of life come crashing in. This is the gospel message. Here Jesus promises to give rest to those who call upon Him. When you feel like you need to bail out, Jesus has your back.

Lord, thank You for providing rest when life becomes too difficult for me to handle on my own.

Encouraging the downhearted and weary!!

Notes

_____
_____
_____
_____
_____
_____

Overhaul – Day 34

By Andrew Starnes – Captain Charlotte Fire Department and FCFInternational member.

""Come to me, all you who are weary and burdened, and I will give you rest."

Matthew 11:28 NIV

As we overhaul, we all know the danger of a hidden fire. In life, if we leave a situation unresolved or we don't properly deal with it, it will 'rekindle', and as in the case of a fire it will cause much greater damage the second time. Overhaul is tough work; it isn't the fun and adrenaline filled experience that you had upon the initial attack of the fire.

In life, overhauling your problem will be even tougher work. You must get to the 'seat of the fire' and remove any charred remains/embers that could cause you further pain later. We often hesitate to finish the job because we are scared of what we may find, being vulnerable, and allowing others to see the dark parts of our lives.

We cannot guarantee that our problems will not rekindle. It is only by giving your life to Jesus that you can be "made a new creation." The pain of inner torment dies when you give it to the one who died for you. He has faced the fire so we don't have to.

Seeking God's Kingdom – Day 35

By Wayne Detzler – International Board Member and Fire Chaplain (Retired)

The crux of Jesus' Sermon on the Mount may be summarized in this verse: "Instead, seek his kingdom, and these things will be added to you." (Luke 12:31 ESV) It turns out that those who place Kingdom matters first, end up with the greatest blessing. "Fear not, little flock, for it is your Father's good pleasure to give you the kingdom. Sell your possessions, and give to the needy. Provide yourselves with moneybags that do not grow old, with a treasure in the heavens that does not fail, where no thief approaches and no moth destroys." (Luke 12:32-3 ESV) After seven decades of my faith life in Christ, I am still struggling to learn this principle: "For where your treasure is, there will your heart be also." (Luke 12:34 ESV)

Notes

_____
_____
_____
_____
_____

Logistics – Day 36

By Craig Duck – President/Missionary

Read Philippians 4:10-20

Encouragement for the day – "And my God will supply all your needs according to His riches in glory in Christ Jesus."

                        Philippians 4:19 Holman Christian Standard

    I was able to have a conversation with my son the other day about the subject of logistics. Seth serves in the United States Army and is assigned to a unit that is tasked with logistics. I love how the military and the fire service are so similar. We talked about the importance of logistics and getting the necessary equipment to the front lines to support the fight. General H. Norman Schwarzkopf, Jr once said that logistics wins wars, and I whole hardily agree. In the fire service if we do not have all of the tools and equipment needed for the emergency we will not be able to mitigate those emergencies and return the community back to a sense of normalcy. Without people working in logistics, our departments would not be able to function.

    The Bible teaches that God uses people to accomplish His will. As we read this passage of scripture, we stumble across an important lesson. Paul is in the ministry, going about the area establishing churches. Paul understood that ministry takes people and resources to change the hearts and minds of the locals and build new churches. The Philippians had evidently given Paul some supplies, and he was thanking them for their support. Paul also reminded the Philippians that because of their kindness God would supply all of their needs as well. We serve a God that knows logistics and takes care of His people by giving us only what we have need of for our ministry to first responders. Remember to thank Him for every supply that He daily provides.

Lord, thank You for every good gift you have given to me.

Encouragement should be a standard operating guideline!!

Notes

_____
_____
_____
_____

Promotions and Blessings – Day 37

By Keith Helms – Battalion Fire Chief (Retired) Charlotte Fire Department and International Board Member

"He will love you, bless you, and multiply you. He will bless your descendants, and the produce of your land—your grain, new wine, and oil—the young of your herds, and the newborn of your flocks, in the land He swore to your fathers that He would give you."

Deuteronomy 7:13 HCS

Firefighters like to get promoted. Moving up in the ranks is one of the many joys of being in the fire service. While we like to get promoted ourselves, we often struggle when someone else is promoted, especially if the other person is not in our close circle or group. When this happens, we often bemoan the fact that someone else got promoted, usually implying that the promotion was not deserved or earned.

It is somewhat like how we view God's blessings, mercy, and grace. Just as we enjoy experiencing the joys of being promoted (typically feeling that we got what we deserved), we enjoy the blessings of God which we also feel are well deserved. When we see that others are being blessed by God, we are inwardly outraged if we feel that the blessings were not earned.

Take a minute to read Luke 4:16-30. In this narrative, Christ spoke in the synagogue about two times when non-Israelites were blessed by God (v. 26-27). The reaction of the listeners? They rose up, took Him out of the city and desired to kill Him. In this passage, God's people were passed over, and the blessings were bestowed on Gentiles who were seen as unworthy. Do we do the same today? How do you respond to God's blessings? When you receive them, do you feel a hint of pride? When others receive them, do you detect an aroma of envy because you feel that God passed over you and favored someone else? Realize that all of us are unworthy on our own. We have never received a blessing from God that was not a result of His grace and His mercy. Examine your heart through the lens of God's word.

Notes:

_____

_____

_____

_____

_____

_____

_____

Wise Speech – Day 38

By Wayne Detzler – International Board Member and Fire Chaplain (Retired)

"The heart of the righteous studies how to answer, but the mouth of the wicked pours forth evil."

Proverbs 15:28 NKJV

Here is a foretaste of the little epistle of James. He will expound the concept of wise speech and urge believers to watch their words. The super significance of speech is James' emphasis when he writes: "If anyone among you thinks he is religious, and does not bridle his tongue but deceives his own heart, this one's religion is useless." (James 1:26 NKJV) Lord, help me today to speak in full awareness of your presence. Amen.

Notes

_____
_____
_____
_____
_____
_____
_____

Spiritually Complacent – Day 39

By Andrew Starnes – Captain Charlotte Fire Department and FCFInternational member.

Have you ever come to a place where your blessed life becomes a schedule, a task list, and then becomes more obligational?

The busy-ness of all the good things in our lives become burdensome.

Why is this so?

We may have forgotten the source of all our blessings. Our service becomes out of habit and not out of eagerness. We tend to lose our focus on Jesus and become weary too easily. Why is this so? Are we asking the wrong questions?

And how do we refresh our spirits?

"Answer the big question of eternity and the little questions of life fall into perspective." Max Lucado

"The difficulty in applying the Bible is not the Bible itself but with our inability to bridge the gap from conceptual to practical. When we don't or can't do this, spiritual dryness, shallowness, and indifference are the results." NIV commentary

If we can then take a fresh look at our lives with a renewed perspective: one of thankfulness! Ingratitude is the bridge that leads away from God. "But those who hope in the Lord will renew their strength." (Isaiah 40:31)

So let's dive into God's Word, seek Him earnestly in prayer, and let us surround ourselves with those who will lead, encourage, and hold us accountable in the faith.

We are Saved! Let's live like it in all the aspects of our life. Let's show our gratitude in all that we do.

Then we can focus on not becoming complacent in our spiritual lives & families. We can live each moment with a thankful heart. We can renew our spirits through Him and look to Him daily, the author and perfecter of our faith.

We will no longer be complacent nor lukewarm but on fire for Christ. This is our calling, and we should surround ourselves with others to help keep our Holy Fire's burning.

Gap Analysis – Day 40

By Craig Duck – President/Missionary

Read Colossians 2:6-14

Encouragement for the day – "See to it that no one takes you captive by philosophy and empty deceit, according to human tradition, according to the elemental spirits of the world, and not according to Christ."

Colossians 2:8 ESV

I was talking to a chief one day when the conversation came up about gap analysis. I had never heard that term before used in the fire service and was interested in the concept. This particular chief worked wildland fires and had worked some of the bigger fires this country has seen. He went on to explain that during big events it is sometimes profitable to take a step back and evaluate how the incident is realistically going. During that time, he will try to identify all of the gaps that are occurring, and then assign people to fill those gaps. This technique has helped him to stay focused on the main goal of extinguishing all of the fire.

The Christian life can sometimes be difficult for those serving in the fire service. It is easy to get caught up in the business of life and then before you know it you have no time for God. During these times it is easy for folks to be carried away by strange philosophies and untrue doctrines. It doesn't happen overnight, but the longer we stay away from God, the easier it can be to fall. If Paul were a chief, he would encourage us to use gap analysis. Take a moment and ensure that every activity, thought and desire aligns with the Bible. Ensure that what you are doing on a daily basis is pleasing to the Lord and not selfish in any way. As you begin to discover gaps in your walk with the Lord, find ways to fill those gaps. Consider attending church more often, reading and studying your Bible, and becoming part of a small group that will help to encourage you. As a Christian firefighter we have been rooted in Christ, and we need to act more like Him on a daily basis.

Lord show me how to please you in everything I do.

Encouraging firefighters and first responders to keep the faith!!

Know For Sure – Day 41

By Wayne Detzler – International Board Member and Fire Chaplain (Retired)

I struggled with faith, especially as I became enmeshed in sinful practices. When Bob Hopkins discipled me, he taught me these two verses first of all. At last, I knew that God really loved me and that He could and would forgive me. "And this is what God has testified: He has given us eternal life, and this life is in his Son. Whoever has the Son [that's Jesus!] has life; whoever does not have God's Son does not have life." (1 John 5:11-12 NLT) And it still works, when I doubt that God can love me.

1. Has there ever been a time in your life when you have placed your faith and trust in Jesus Christ?

2. What sins do you struggle with?

To learn more about having a right relationship with God, go to our website and check out God's plan for Christian firefighters in our training section.

www.fellowshipofchristianfirefighters.org

Crawling Down the Hallway – Day 42
By Craig Duck – President/Missionary

Read James 1:12-18

Encouragement for the day – "Blessed is the man who endures temptation; for when he has been approved, he will receive the crown of life which the Lord has promised to those who love Him."

James 1:12 NKJV

    One of the most difficult tasks a firefighter must accomplish is to crawl down the hallway of a building that is on fire. Several times in my career the decision was made to crawl down the hallway because there was a lot to be gained. The risk was worth the effort because the fire at the end of the hallway needed to be extinguished to protect the rescue effort that was underway. As we worked our way to the room that was on fire the heat was intense, to the point of almost making us give up on our objective. Once we reached that room, it was extinguished and we could celebrate our victory.

    God has never promised Christian firefighters that it would be easy in this life once we become saved. There are those who are quick to tell you that our belief in Christ should produce wealth and prosperity, but that is just not the case. The more we do for the cause of Christ the more we will be under attack by the evil one. His goal is to get us to quit and give up on the tasks that God has given to us. Like crawling down a hallway is paramount to the task of extinguishing a fire, the Christian firefighter must endure the temptation to quit if he/she wants to succeed in the Christian faith. God has promised us the He will be with us the entire time, and provide us with His peace. John reminds us in I John 16:33; "I have said these things to you, that in me you may have peace. In the world, you will have tribulation. But take heart; I have overcome the world." If you are struggling today because you feel under attack, I encourage you to take it to God in prayer. God can not only answer your prayers for help but can provide you with a peace that the world does not understand.

Lord when I feel like giving up I thank you for being right there beside me in my time of need.

Encouragement, take some and share some!!

A Leadership Prayer – Day 43

By Andrew Starnes – Captain Charlotte Fire Department and FCFInternational member

Lord, let me be first to awake so I may lead my family.
And last to the bed as to ensure their safety.

Let, me be the first to admit when I am wrong.
And let me remain humble throughout all my life.

Let me be the first to speak up for the poor, the helpless, & the broken.
And erase my sinful pride so I may not become pious and outspoken.

Let me be the first to read Your word and pray.
And let me be the last to study Your word at the end of each day.

Let me be the first to consider Your ways.
And let me be the last to fall back into my old sinful ways.

Let me be the first to stay disciplined.
And let me be the last to leave a hurting friend.

Let me be the first to offer all that I have.
And help me to lift up others whose hearts are sad.

Let me be the first to open my heart, my home, and my wallet.
And let me be the last to expose another's faults.

Let me be thy servant, committed to your plans
And let me not forget that my sins were washed by the blood of your hands.

Let me remember your words when I desire to be first in this life:

"Not so with you. Instead, whoever wants to become great among you must be your servant, and whoever wants to be first must be slave of all. For even the Son of Man did not come to be served, but to serve, and to give his life as a ransom for many."

Mark 10:43-45 NIV

Keep my heart filled with your spirit, my life available to serve, and humble me so I may never be far from your sight.

In Christ's name, I pray

Time Sensitive – Day 44

By Wayne Detzler – International Board Member and Fire Chaplain (Retired)

Pastor Steve reminded us yesterday that each person stands face to face with God. Jesus wept on that first Palm Sunday because people had missed "the TIME of God's coming." (Luke 19:44 NIV) Revival is a special "time of God's coming." Speaking at a conference recently, an attendee accosted me. He was disturbed by fringe people in the emerging revival. As a result, he seemed to be missing out on God's time. The New Testament uses the word, KAIROS, for this time. It is opportunity! Revived people are those who have recognized God's Time. Let's not miss it!

1. How can you better minister in God's timing?

2. In what ways do you easily become impatient?

Door Control – Day 45

By Andrew Starnes – Captain Charlotte Fire Department and FCFInternational member.

In the fire service today, it is alive with research, development, and forward thinking leaders helping to bring positive change to the world.

One such topic is Anti-Ventilation. By controlling the fires air flow, we thereby control its growth. As firefighters, we often start off our fire service journey as free-burning "fuel regulated" fires that seem inextinguishable.
But then life happens:

Our passion for what we do becomes choked down by negativity, amount of other fires we have burning (too many commitments) and need more air (encouragement, time, and energy).

We have become vent limited; our 'fire' has reached a decay phase.

We have let others that are too weak to follow their dreams discourage ours.

Consider this:

"Ask and it will be given to you, seek and you will find; knock and the door will be opened to you. For everyone asks receives; the one who seeks finds, and the one who knocks the door will be opened."

Matthew 7:7-8

Remember that as we journey through the fires of our lives, when all other doors are closed, one remains, open-the-door into the presence of God through prayer.
Force the door open with the most powerful forcible entry tool there is:

Prayer

Notes

_____
_____
_____
_____
_____
_____
_____
_____

Engaging the Pump – Day 46
By Craig Duck – President/Missionary

Read Matthew 28:16-20

Encouragement for the day – "Go ye therefore, and teach all nations, baptizing them in the name of the Father, and of the Son, and of the Holy Ghost:"

Mathew 28:19 KJV

Fire service pumps have come a long way since the colonial days of America. In the early days, water was delivered to the fire in buckets brought forth through hard work from the water source to the fire. Then the hand-operated fire pump was introduced into the fire service, which still took a lot of manpower to get the water out of the hole. Today we have a centrifugal pump that is capable of delivering large quantities of water with little effort. The pump utilizes the same drive shaft that powers the great diesel motor which carries the apparatus to the scene. Once on location the driver simply puts the apparatus in park and engages the pump by utilizing a transfer switch. Without transferring the power from the engine to the pump to engage the fire pump, it will simply sit there accomplishing nothing. Once the pump is engaged water can be delivered to the seat of the fire, and the fire quickly extinguished.

Christian first responders have been commanded by God to make disciples. This command was given by Jesus after the resurrection and before returning to the Father in heaven. Jesus spent a lifetime teaching His disciples how a Godly man or woman is to conduct themselves in a fallen world. Jesus reminds His disciples that they have been authorized to make disciples by God Himself and that they have been equipped through the teaching and example that Jesus has given them. The next step for Christians is to get engaged in the battle. Those Christian first responders who choose not to get engaged are as useful as the pump that goes to a fire and idly sits in front of a burning building. God wants us to get engaged, being obedient to the command of making disciples, and as we go through life share what we have learned and know about God with others. When the Christian first responder gets engaged in discipleship, God promises to be with him or her, until the end. Are you engaged in the battle?

Lord, thank You for Your promises that are true and encourage me to make disciples.

Encouraging first responders to keep the faith!!

Obligation – Day 47

By Wayne Detzler – Fire Chaplain (Retired) and International Board Member

"For I have a great sense of obligation to people in both the civilized world and the rest of the world, to the educated and uneducated alike."

Rom. 1:14 NLT

Paul took his role as a witness very seriously. He spoke of it as an "obligation," and this continually amazes me. The God of the universe chooses people like us to be His witness on this earth. Jesus says we are lights in a dark world. (Matt. 5:16) So, wherever we are, let's shine for Jesus today.

1. How can you better shine your light in the Department God has called you to?

2. What prevents you from shining your light?

3. How does it make you feel to be chosen by God?

The Cost of the Fire Service – Day 48

By Andrew Starnes – Captain Charlotte Fire Department and FCFInternational member.

Another week has flown by, and I am reminded how blessed I am to return home safely from another many hours away from home. But, many times in life we work these long hours without thought of the great cost that is paid on our behalf in our absence.

For example, in this one week consisting of 168 hours, I will have missed over 100 hours of it with my family. Double shifts and teaching all seem to fall into the same week, but those hours I missed also consisted of:

My wife taking our daughter to church alone... / My wife taking our daughter to school all five days this week all while she has to work as well... / My wife setting up a babysitter for two of these days where our work schedules overlap... / My wife running the necessary errands, keeping our household running, paying bills, preparing meals, and keeping up with family concerns.... / My wife getting our daughter to her Wednesday night church group (AWANAS)

My wife does this each week and so much more all the time. She gives of herself and sacrifices her time (and many times her sleep) to get it all done. So when each of us work a long week and we return home tired (and often frustrated) we need to remember the great cost that is being paid on our behalf.

Remember that our wives are often tired and carry the same burdens we carry. Remember that our wives our modeling Jesus' sacrificial love to us in their daily acts of commitment to our marriages.

Remember the words of Proverbs 31:10-11

"Who can find a capable wife?
  She is far more precious than jewels.
  The heart of her husband trusts in her,
  And he will not lack anything good."

Give thanks, this day that we have wives that are capable and precious to us. And make sure that they know how much we appreciate them. Let's show them our love every day through our words, actions, texts, and more.

Give thanks, each day for a spouse that completes us, works with us, and puts up with us through it all.

Re-tone Company 1 – Day 49
By Craig Duck – President/Missionary

Read Luke 10:1-12

Encouragement for the day – "Therefore said he unto them, The harvest truly is great, but the labourers are few: pray ye therefore the Lord of the harvest, that he would send forth labourers into his harvest."

Luke 10:2 KJV

    During a daytime response for our little volunteer fire department, we were shorthanded. The call came in for a school bus that was on its side with the driver trapped. As I sat in the fire truck waiting for others to come, I hoped that the dispatcher was wrong. I marked Engine 11 enroute with 1 and headed for the scene. The responding chief heard the amount of people he had responding to the accident and asked the dispatcher to re-tone company 1 in hopes that more people would respond. Fortunately, when we arrived on scene there were no children on the bus and the driver, who was unhurt, was able to get out.

    We read in today's Bible reading the story of Jesus appointing and sending out 70 people to proclaim the message that the kingdom of God was at hand. His strategy was simple, send them out in pairs and have them go from house to house. It is interesting to me that God always uses people to partner with Him to expand the Kingdom. He could use other means to accomplish His goals, but God uses those who are willing to get involved. Isn't it amazing that with all of the professing Christian firefighters we have, how few are willing to give all of their effort for the cause of Christ in the fire service. Perhaps we should begin to re-tone for more Christian firefighters to get actively involved; "therefore pray the Lord of the harvest to send out laborers into His harvest."

Lord thank you for choosing to use me to proclaim the good news of Jesus Christ. May I give of my all today for you.

Encouragement starts with you and spreads like wildfire!!

Notes

_____
_____
_____
_____
_____

Send Us – Day 50

By Wayne Detzler – Fire Chaplain (Retired) and International Board Member

"Send us around the world with news of your saving power and your plan for" all people."

Psalm 67:2 Living Bible

From the heart of God, the psalmist senses a passion for the whole world. This divine energy has catapulted generations of missionaries across the world to share God's saving power. As we look forward to summer 2013, Mark and Cathy plan to visit missionaries in Brazil. Carol and Scott plan to minister in Rwanda. Several of our grandchildren have undertaken missionary projects either at home or in other countries. God promises to bless this effort when he inspires the psalmist to write: "God, even our God will bless us, and people from the remotest lands will worship him." (Psalm 67:6-7 Living Bible)

Psalm 67

For the choir director: A song. A psalm, to be accompanied by stringed instruments.

May God be merciful and bless us.
May his face smile with favor on us. Interlude
May your ways be known throughout the earth,
your saving power among people everywhere.
May the nations praise you, O God.
Yes, may all the nations praise you.
Let the whole world sing for joy,
because you govern the nations with justice
and guide the people of the whole world. Interlude
May the nations praise you, O God.
Yes, may all the nations praise you.
Then the earth will yield its harvests,
and God, our God, will richly bless us.
Yes, God will bless us,
and people all over the world will fear him.

1. Where do you feel God leading you to share His Good News?

Going Viral – Day 51
By Craig Duck – President/Missionary

Read Acts 8:1-13

Encouragement for the day – "Therefore they that were scattered abroad went everywhere preaching the word."
Acts 8:4 KJV

    As I was coming down the stairs the other day at Engine Company 11 in Washington, DC, I heard a lot of laughter coming out of the office area. When I rounded the corner, I saw all of the young firefighters watching videos on the computer. These young firefighters started out watching some training videos to be better firefighters. By the time it was over, they were watching silly clips of random people. Some of the videos were funny, people doing things they should have known better not to do. One of the young firefighters blurted out "it's hard to believe, but some of these videos have gone viral." Viral is the term for a video that spreads quickly, sometimes to millions of viewers in a matter of days.

    This is not a new phenomenon. We read in Acts that after Stephen, a leader in the early church was stoned for his faith the church was persecuted. The young Christians were then spread out to other parts of the country. Rather than these Christians being silenced, we read that they went everywhere preaching the good news of Jesus Christ.

God allowed the gospel to go "viral." Those of us who know Jesus Christ as our Lord and Savior should not keep the good news of eternal life to ourselves. Even in difficult times and challenging circumstances in the fire service, we should keep on telling others about Jesus.

Lord, give me the strength to share my faith with another firefighter today.

Encouraging one another in the fire service!!

Notes

_____
_____
_____
_____
_____
_____
_____
_____

Acting Officers – Day 52

By Keith Helms – Battalion Fire Chief (Retired) Charlotte Fire Department and International Board Member

Most fire departments want to be known for their aggressive, interior firefighters. They train and equip their members to safely enter a burning structure to fight the battle at its source. Typically, the Command Staff knows who they can rely on; they also know the firefighters that prefer to stay outside. While I acknowledge that there are times when you have to go defensive, the problem is that there are firefighters who never want to go inside. They refuse to face the challenge of getting close enough to engage in the battle.

As an IC, I was fortunate to have a battalion (Batt. 4-A) of officers and firefighters that could be counted on to aggressively fight the fire. Going defensive was not the predominate strategy. Getting inside was always the desired approach. Time after time, the crews entered the structure; and time after time, the fire was controlled without further damage to the structure.

We all face a similar problem with sin. Many prefer to deal with sin without dealing with the source. The real problem resides inside. Matthew 23:25- 28 illustrates the difference between an interior attack and an external attack on sin.

"Woe to you, scribes and Pharisees, hypocrites! For you clean the outside of the cup and the plate, but inside they are full of greed and self-indulgence. You blind Pharisee! First clean the inside of the cup and the plate, that the outside also may be clean. Woe to you, scribes and Pharisees, hypocrites! For you are like whitewashed tombs, which outwardly appear beautiful, but within are full of dead people's bones and all uncleanness. So you also outwardly appear righteous to others, but within you are full of hypocrisy and lawlessness."

Failing to be an aggressive, interior "sinfighter" will result in superficial changes. Christ desires followers who will fight sin at its core. He wants changed hearts. His disciples are not afraid to face the interior battle. They are empowered by the Holy Spirit to attack the enemy (Romans 8:12-17), just as good firefighters are trained and equipped for interior firefighting. Face the enemy interiorly; that is where you will find the victory.

For further study:

Ps. 51:6-12; 139:23-24 • Prov. 16:2; 17:3 • 1 Sam. 16:7 • Jer. 11:20; 17:9-10; 20:12 • Amos 5:21-24 • Luke 19:15 • 1 Cor. 4:5 • 2 Cor. 10:7 • Heb. 4:12-13

Whirled Away – Day 53

By Wayne Detzler – International Board Member and Fire Chaplain (Retired)

"When the storms of life come, the wicked are whirled away, but the godly have a lasting foundation."

Proverbs 10:25 NLT

The writer of Proverbs paints a powerful picture from flash floods that sweep all in their way. The storms of life provide broadcast news footage from near and far. Every day we learn of new threats and disasters. In the Sermon on the Mount Jesus re-packaged this proverb: "Anyone who listens to my teaching and follows it is wise, like a person who builds a house on solid rock. Though the rain comes in torrents and the floodwaters rise, and the winds beat against that house, it won't collapse because it is built on bedrock." (Matthew 7:24-5 NLT) Lord Jesus, help me today to build my life on your Word. Amen.

1. How has God helped you through the storms of life in the past?

2. What Bible verses comfort you during difficult days?

Acting Officers – Day 54

By Craig Duck – President/Missionary

Read James 4:7-10

Encouragement for the day – "Draw near to God and He will draw near to you. Cleanse your hands, you sinners; and purify your hearts, you double-minded."

James 4:8 NKJV

Years ago, before I was promoted to the rank of sergeant in the District of Columbia Fire Department, I was called upon to act as one. An acting officer doesn't receive any increase in pay but is required to fulfill all of the duties of an officer. The actor rides the front seat of the apparatus and makes all of the decisions for the company on emergencies. As information is received, it must be prioritized and acted upon to resolve the crisis at hand. During the day as administrative situations would arise, the acting officer must handle them as if he/she were the actual officer. While I spent time waiting to get promoted, I learned a lot about dealing with personalities, handling emergencies and making decisions to better the company I was working with.

    The Bible contains truth that is relevant to today's Christian firefighters. Once the information is received via personal Bible reading, studying or listening to a sermon the hearer then has a choice to make. Will I act upon what is said, or will I continue as before? It is essential for us to act upon the truth of the Bible. We cannot force others to believe; we simply must afford them an opportunity to act upon that truth as well. When a truth is brought home, don't allow it to pass without any change. Confess your sins to God and allow His power to rest upon your life. So often we firefighters attempt to handle every emergency in our lives under our power and in our way. God desires for us to draw nearer to Him and follow all of His ways.

Lord, thank You for helping me through tough and difficult times in my life, may my life glorify You today.

Encouragement, the art of lifting people up!!

www.fellowshipofchristianfirefighters.org

Lightweight Construction – Day 55

By Andrew Starnes – Captain Charlotte Fire Department and FCFInternational member.

In the fire service today, we are trained to understand the dangers of lightweight construction's performance under fire conditions. Because of our training, we know that despite a building's strong appearance on the outside, we are full aware of its structural weaknesses such as engineered lumber, gusset plates, I-Joists, and more. These components are lighter, cheaper, and allows the builder to complete the building faster. But appearances can be deceiving.

Consider the application of 'light-weight construction' for our lives: We must ask ourselves if our values and core beliefs are either built upon the solid rock of Christ or are they built without any foundation and tied together with weak and lightweight components that will fail under the fires of adversity.

"But the one who hears my words and does not put them into practice is like a man who built a house on the ground without a foundation. The moment the torrent struck that

house, it collapsed, and its destructions was complete."
Luke 6: 48-49

We are called to build our lives upon the strong rock of Jesus Christ. I have found that in my life when I have tried to stand on my strength without Jesus that I quickly collapsed as the torrents of life struck me down. I also found that when my beliefs were questioned that I wavered and compromised my beliefs based upon social & political pressures.

Jesus asks us "Why do you call me, 'Lord, Lord, and do not do what I say?"

So, let us consider whether or not our 'spiritual houses' are well built?

"As for everyone who comes to me and hears my words & put them into practice I will show you what they are like:

They are like a man building a house, who dug down deep and laid the foundation upon the rock. When a flood came, the torrent struck the house but could not shake it, because it was well built." (Luke 6:46-47).
So, let us continue to ensure that our houses are 'well built' and stay upon the unshakable rock of Jesus Christ.

Loneliness...Blessing or Curse? – Day 56

By Keith Helms – Battalion Fire Chief (Retired) Charlotte Fire Department and International Board Member

The fire service is known for its brotherhood, its camaraderie. Firefighters are a part of a family. If this is true, then why do so many firefighters suffer with loneliness? Why would someone be lonely if they are a part of a unique family?

The reality is, if we are living in truth that loneliness is inevitable this side of heaven. Man was created by The Triune God for perfect relationships. However, because no human relationship will ever be free from the effects of sin, even the best human relationships are incapable of insulating us from loneliness. A good marriage, a great fire company, a Christ-centered church...they all will come short of perfection. Loneliness reminds us that we are not home. We are pilgrims passing through this world (Heb. 11:13; 1 Pet. 2:11). However, a sense of loneliness can be a gift from God. Loneliness opens the door to relating to God on a level that no other person can provide. It invites us to explore our heart level need to seek Him over anything or anyone else.

When a firefighter experiences the pains of loneliness, he/she has three options:

1. Despair or dying inside. He/she disengages from others in an attempt to avoid involvement or disappointment.
2. Fight to maintain a sense of control. He/she numbs the pain with false intimacy which often is seen in addiction to pornography. He/she may have many relationships, but they are most often superficial. Facebook is a good example.
3. Acknowledge that nothing in this world can satisfy the heart level longing that we have for God. He/she accepts that the completeness of our relationship with God can never be fully experienced this side of heaven. He/she believes that Christ is all that he needs to persevere and to walk in holiness.

Loneliness reminds us that we were created for a perfect relationship. We will have perfect intimacy in heaven; let that promise sustain you through the difficulties of this life. Loneliness draws us to the reality that our hope for a completely perfect relationship will be fulfilled in heaven. It is this hope that has the power to sustain you through the darkest days in this world. It is often in those seasons of loneliness that God does is greatest work in the lives of His children.

Meditate on these words from Elizabeth Elliot: "We have noted that aloneness was not a painful thing until sin entered the world. Loneliness now means pain. The other aspect of loneliness, solitude, need not mean pain. It may mean glory. Loneliness is a wilderness, but through receiving it as a gift, accepting it from the hand of God and offering it back to Him with thanksgiving, it may become a pathway to holiness, to glory and to God Himself."

1. How have dealt with loneliness in the past?

2. Has it helped or hurt the situation?

3. List Bible verses that would provide you with comfort during times of loneliness.

Junior Firefighters – Day 57
By Craig Duck – President/Missionary

Read Luke 2:41-52

Encouragement for the day – "And Jesus increased in wisdom and stature, and in favor with God and men."

Luke 2:52 NKJV

When I was growing up in Upstate New York, I used to hang out at the firehouse with my dad. I looked forward to every Saturday and the different adventures my dad, and I would experience at the station. Hanging out with firefighters taught me a lot about the commitment it takes to serve. As I became older, I was able to join a junior fire department in a neighboring community. Junior firefighters are a way for young folks to get involved in the fire service while learning the skills necessary to become a firefighter. Today it takes a lot of time, effort, and training classes to become a firefighter and a good "Juniors" program will prepare folks for service.

Jesus, the Son of God, came to the earth as a lowly child in a manger. As we read about the life of the Son of Man, we learn that He grew (Luke 2:40) just like you and I did. Luke gives an interesting story when Jesus was just 12 years of age. Jesus's parents, Mary and Joseph, went on their annual long trip to the Temple for the Passover celebration. On the way back they discovered that Jesus was missing and went back to look for Him. They found Jesus in the Temple listening to the teachers and asking them questions. Jesus made it a priority to be in God's House and to learn more about God's Word. Shouldn't we as firefighters desire the same for our lives? And shouldn't we instill the same priorities in the lives of our family? Take time this week to go to a church that teaches the truth of God's Word.

Lord, help me to make going to church a priority in my life.

Encouraging first responders to keep the faith!!

Notes

_____
_____
_____
_____

Weaned on a Dill Pickle – Day 58

By Wayne Detzler – International Board Member and Fire Chaplain (Retired)

"You made me so happy, GOD I saw your work, and I shouted for joy. How magnificent your work, GOD! How profound your thoughts!"

Psalm 92:4 The Message

Scripture sizzles with references to joy. One of the dominant characteristics of believers in the Lord is joy. Unfortunately, some miss the point. The great preacher Vance Havner said: "Some Christians look like they were weaned on a dill pickle." So, the point is this. Today tell your face to show the joy of the Lord. Because His joy is our strength! (Nehemiah 8:10)

1. What prevents you from having real joy in your life?

2. What actions can you take to daily ensure your face shows the joy of the Lord.

Who's in Command – Day 59

By Andrew Starnes – Captain Charlotte Fire Department and FCFInternational member.

Sorrow and memories of loved ones that have passed on can overwhelm our hearts at times. As firefighters, we don't like to admit that we lose control of ourselves as we are a model of control amidst chaos to others.

We have before us a decision to make in these conflagrations of emotions:

We can embrace and face the pain.

-or-

We can suppress the pain only to have it rekindle once again in our lives causing, even more, collateral damage.

So many people are touched by the actions of first responders today. Lives are saved, fears are calmed, and normalcy is restored amidst crisis.

We have an often untapped and underused resource for ourselves when we need rescue. His name is Jesus Christ. He goes to the Father on our behalf. And He understands!

Consider the fact that there are also those who never stop praying for us:

"Since the day we heard of you, we have not stopped praying for you." 1 Colossians 1:3

We will face moments of emotional instability and pain but dear friends we are not alone. Our brothers & sisters lift us up in prayer, and Jesus Christ hears those prayers!

He offers us all the "peace that passes understanding" which is peace in our hearts while the storms of our lives rage on. As a firefighter trusts in those around them amidst the flames, so we must put an even greater trust in our true Incident Commander: Jesus Christ.

Even if we have accepted Him as our Savior, many of us have not let Him take Command of our hearts. Let us not freelance anymore with our hearts & lives. Let us all put our trust and hope in the one who has already rescued us from the greatest fire.

Pulling the Fire Alarm – Day 60
By Craig Duck – President/Missionary

Read Psalm 116:1-7

Encouragement for the day – "I love the Lord, for he heard my voice; he heard my cry for mercy. Because he turned his ear to me, I will call on him as long as I live."

Psalm 116:1-2 NIV

Firefighters don't typically pull a fire alarm. During my time as a firefighter, there has only been several times that a fire has occurred and the alarm was not pulled when we arrived. As soon as the first firefighters passed by a fire alarm pull station, one pulled it to alert the rest of the residents in the building. The fire alarm system was designed for residents to be able to alert other residents of the danger of fire so everyone can escape safely. Most systems today go directly to a dispatch center who then contacts the fire department for help.

When firefighters have a personal emergency, where can they turn for help? Today's firefighters face new types of challenges and struggles that can easily affect who they are. That is why we have seen an increase in substance abuse, firefighter discipline cases, and suicide. God provides hope to firefighters when it seems like nobody else cares. The Psalmist cried out to God, who heard his cry for help. David had experienced many battles in his life, and when he felt like death was knocking at his door, he reached out to God for help. You can do the same thing David did for whatever you are going through right now. God is merciful and loving and desires to be there for you no matter what. If you are struggling today with something, sound the alarm to God and allow Him to come to your aid.

Lord thank you for loving me so much that you sent your Son Jesus Christ to die to pay the penalty for my sins.

Sometimes we all need a little ENCOURAGEMENT!!!

1. How can you better encourage firefighters who need your help?

2. Who are some people in your station whom you can pray for today?

Make the Call – Day 61

By Andrew Starnes – Captain Charlotte Fire Department and FCFInternational member.

As firefighters, we see pain, tragedy, and death on a regular basis. But then those experiences come to us when:

A close friend dies suddenly... / A family member becomes very sick... / A loved one betrays our trust... / An injury causes a major setback... / A child dies... / A friend commits suicide...

Then with all of the pain around us, those years of trauma erupt to the surface of our souls. We break into pieces and anxiety grips out heart.

What then shall we do?
Our roles become reversed. Those who look to others in their moments of distress are now themselves distressed and in need of rescue.

We Cry out:

God, "Do not be far from me for trouble is near and there is no one to help" (Psalm 22:11).

Let's not bury our emotions; let them pour out in passionate and overwhelming pleas to God. Call upon Him, our families, and the brotherhood.

Be honest in these painful moments and realize we are human beings who need help to. This is not a sign of weakness but courage and strength.

Remember that God's word tells us: "For he had not despised or scorned the suffering of the afflicted one; he has not hidden his face from him but has listened to his cry for help" (Psalm 22:24).

God is waiting on us to cry out. He holds the answers we seek. He holds the comfort we so desperately need. He gives the peace that passes all understanding to those who trust in Him. But we must make the call.

As we respond to the call of those who need help in a crisis, let us remember that God stands ready to respond to the calls of our heart. If only we would just "cast our cares upon him for he cares for us." (1 Peter 5:7).

Call upon God today!

Accident With Entrapment – Day 62

By Craig Duck – President/Missionary

Read Joshua 24:14-21

Encouragement for the day – "And if it seems evil to you to serve the Lord, choose for yourselves this day whom you will serve, whether the gods which your fathers served that were on the other side of the River, or the gods of the Amorites, in whose land you dwell. But as for me and my house, we will serve the Lord."

Joshua 24:15 NKJV

The other day we were dispatched to an accident with entrapment. As we were responding to the scene, we made sure everyone knew their assignment. I was assigned patient evaluation; another firefighter was assigned to operate the tools while the officer evaluated the incident. The driver of the vehicle made some bad choices while driving down the road which led to his truck going off the road into a ditch and flipping over. The operation was successful as the patient was removed from the vehicle and flown to a nearby hospital.

Joshua and the people of God had finally made it to the Promised Land and Joshua was giving them a little pep talk. He reminded them that it was God that had safely guided them along the way and provided for all of their needs. Joshua also reminded the Israelites that some of their fathers had chosen not to follow after the one true God but chose to serve idols. In life, firefighters can be easily distracted from serving God. Every day we have to make choices that not only affect us but others around us. Many of those choices turn our hearts and minds away from serving God and trap us or entangle us. If you have made some bad choices in life, it is not too late to turn things around. God can extricate us from our current circumstances and allow us the opportunity to serve Him. Joshua made that choice when he stated to everyone "as for me and my house, we will serve the Lord, " and you can make the same decision. Learn more about serving the Lord by going to our website; www.fellowshipofchristianfirefighters.org

Lord, thank You for forgiving me of my sins; help me this week to refresh my commitment to serve You no matter what the circumstances.

Encouragement, everyone needs a little from time to time!!

Unbeatable Joy – Day 63

By Wayne Detzler – International Board Member and Fire Chaplain (Retired)

"The joy of the Lord is your strength."

Nehemiah 8:10 NLT

Religion does not work. Religious routine produces a parade of people, whose faces look like an advertisement for gravity. Awakening rekindles joy in believers. This joy is like an incandescent bulb--it glows from the inside out. As Paul put it: "Rejoice in the Lord always, and again I say rejoice." (Phil. 4:4) In this way, we "let our light shine." (Matt. 5:16) Laughter is not only the best medicine; it's also a great witness for the joy of the Lord.

1. How can you rekindle the joy you once had?

2. What situations cause you to be discouraged?

3. How can you avoid those situations?

Earning a Spot in Heaven – Day 64
By Craig Duck – President/Missionary

Read Titus 3:1-8

Encouragement for the day – "not by works of righteousness which we have done, but according to His mercy He saved us, through the washing of regeneration and renewing of the Holy Spirit,"

Titus 3:5 NKJV

    I started working out yesterday to earn a spot on the competition team this year. Only the best are allowed to compete. I know it is a little early, but I wanted to ensure that I am physically fit when practice time begins. Since I have retired, it is much easier to gain weight and get out of shape. When I worked in the District of Columbia Fire Department, I had the option to use the weight room at least every four days, and I frequently took advantage of that luxury. So I joined a local gym and yesterday began getting back in shape, hoping to earn that coveted spot on the team.

    Many folks are misinformed on how to earn a spot in heaven. The Apostle Paul reminded us that we are not capable of earning a spot in heaven; it is only by the mercy of God that we are saved. Our works can in no way pay the penalty for the sins we have committed. Only through our faith in Jesus Christ and the completed work on the cross can we obtain eternal life. Any other attempt falls short. Having a right relationship with our heavenly Father is as simple as ABC. A – Acknowledge you're a sinner and repent (Romans 3:23, Romans 6:23). B – Believe in Jesus as the Son of God (Acts 16:31). C – Confess your sins to God and your faith in Jesus as Lord and Savior (I John 1:9, Romans 10:9). The new life that comes through a saving faith in Jesus is the only way to heaven, and it's open to anyone.

Lord thank you for saving my soul and allowing me eternal life. Help me today to share this good news with my friends in the fire service.

Encouraging firefighters to keep the faith!

Notes

_____
_____
_____
_____
_____

I Remember the Days of Old – Day 65

By Keith Helms – Battalion Fire Chief (Retired) Charlotte Fire Department and International Board Member

"And we know that in all things God works for the good of those who love him, who have been called according to his purpose."

Romans 8:28 NIV

When a few retirees get together, it is almost inevitable that you will eventually begin to hear the stories of "how it used to be." You will hear about the fires that were hotter; the chiefs that were meaner; the firefighters that were braver and tougher; and the practical jokes that were funnier.

I hope that this is not a bad thing because I find myself doing it on a regular basis. It is good for us to remember the old days. Remembering the past helps us to have a better perspective of the present and the future. This is especially true in our spiritual walk. Psalm 143:5 says, "I will remember the days of old; I will meditate on all Your works." Meditating on the past provides the opportunity to see the works of God in our lives. By looking at the past, we can see the evidences of the sovereign will of God. This should greatly influence how we see the present and the future. The past gives us the confidence to trust Him today and tomorrow, no matter the circumstances that we are facing. The scriptures encourage us to remember God (Deuteronomy 8; Psalm 42, Psalm 63, Psalm 20:7, Isaiah 46:8-9); to think deeply about Him and His nature. As believers, this is the basis of our hope. We can look beyond the seemingly insurmountable mountains of this world, and we trust in Him and His love and goodness.

When you gather together with other firefighters, enjoy the stories of "how it used to be." But your deepest joy should be in the delight of telling the stories of God. The stories of the past validate the truth that "... all things work together for good to those who love God, to those who are the called according to His purpose (Romans 8:28).

1. How has God helped you through difficult times in the past?

2. When was the last time you shared how God has blessed you with others?

B.L.E.V.E. – Day 66
By Craig Duck – President/Missionary

Read Psalm 119:1-11

Encouragement for the day – "With my whole heart I seek you; let me not wander from your commandments! I have stored up your word in my heart, that I might not sin against you."

Psalm 119:10-11 ESV

When was the first time you heard the term B.L.E.V.E.? When I was a recruit firefighter for the Washington, DC Fire Department, we watched a video on that topic. As I recall the instructors used a video of a firefighter that was operating a ladder pipe at a train fire. One of the rail cars that was loaded with a flammable liquid was heated to the point where the boiling liquid was released from a weakened portion of the tank, and the escaping vapors immediately exploded. The fire service loves to use acronyms, and this was one of the first ones to come out. B.L.E.V.E stands for boiling liquid expanding vapor explosion.

Christian firefighters should adopt the practice of making acronyms out of little sayings that will help us to remember Biblical principles. As an example, we could ask other Christian firefighters if they are a B.L.E.V.E. type of Christian. This new term could stand for Bible loving encouraging and victorious evangelical. The first part of Psalm 119 introduces us to the concept of truly loving the word of God. The Psalmist uses terms like walking in the law of the Lord, seeking God with our whole heart, and remaining upright through God's righteous rules. While this little acronym may seem a little peculiar, it helps us to focus on the main thing; loving God and keeping His commandments. We can accomplish this task when we regularly read and study our Bibles. How about you, are you a Bible loving encouraging and victorious evangelical? If not, start today by reading your Bible.

Lord help me today to make time for the important things of life today, reading your word.

Encouraging first responders to keep the faith!!

1. In what specific way can you love God and keep His commandment this week?

Joyful Integrity – Day 67

By Wayne Detzler – International Board Member and Fire Chaplain (Retired)

"Joyful are people of integrity, who follow the instructions of the LORD. Joyful are those who obey his laws and search for him with all their hearts."

Psalm 119:1-2 NLT

The Beatitudes of the New Testament are part of Jesus' Sermon on the Mount. The pattern is as old as the psalms. Notice the link between integrity and living according to the Word of God. As we move into a new role with Black Rock Church's prayer team, it is my heart cry that our lives will be marked by absolute integrity. But also, it is my prayer that we will spread the joy of those who "search for him with all their hearts!"

1. How have you struggled with integrity issues this past year?

2. How can you better set yourself up for success in the future?

Filling Tankers – Day 68

By Craig Duck – President/Missionary

Read Habakkuk 2:12-16

Encouragement for the day – "For the earth will be filled with the knowledge of the Lord's glory, as the waters cover the sea."

Habakkuk 2:14 Holman Christian Standard

In the country, there isn't a hydrant on every corner. To ensure constant water supply, fire departments must utilize tankers in their operations. The number of tankers needed depends on the distance between the incident and the water source, the time it takes to fill and offload a tanker and the amount of water needed. Some departments are good at setting up a rural water supply system, and I love to watch them do it. It takes an operations plan that is tried and tested, along with firefighters who are capable of setting all the equipment up promptly. Filling the tankers with water is one of the crucial components of the plan and must be accomplished with precision to ensure companies don't run out of water.

The book of Habakkuk is not widely read today. Habakkuk was a prophet of God who was used to let Judah know of the coming judgment because of their unrepentant hearts and their open rebellion. While Habakkuk did not fully understand God's plan for His people, he did fully trust in God's wisdom. God still rules over the whole earth today, including the fire service, and uses whomever He chooses to accomplish His purposes. Christian firefighters are called to fully trust God no matter what the circumstances around us may be. Rather than complaining about the ungodly things going on in the world today we should be diligently working to spread the knowledge of God's great love for us. Is your tank empty? Fill it by regularly reading the Bible and then share it with others.

    Lord, I thank you today that you are still in control. Though the world around me may be falling apart, you have everything under control.

Encouragement should be a standard operating guideline!!

Asking Why – Day 69

By Andrew Starnes – Captain Charlotte Fire Department and FCFInternational member.

Firefighters often face situations with terrible circumstances, tragic outcomes, and despite our efforts, many are lost. We often carry the scars of that one call we will never forget buried in our hearts for all our days. It weighs on us, dims our outlook, and begins to affect our daily lives. Then when hard times come in our lives, we cry out to God in anguish and despair asking the simple yet profound question "Why God?"

Many have turned away from God in their darkest moments, but have we considered this:

"When belief in God becomes difficult, the tendency is to turn away from Him; but in heaven's name to what?" G.K. Chesterton

We find ourselves as firefighters in a paradox, a state of self-contradiction, where if we looked at our lives from an outsider's point of view we may see things differently.

The paradox is this: we as emergency responders train to handle any situation, at any time, with a moment's notice, and stay calm in face of chaos and uncertainty. We have received countless hours of training and education that has prepared our mind and body but have we forgotten to train the very foundation of ourselves?

Have we prepared our hearts?

Consider the life of Jesus just before his crucifixion. He was preparing the hearts of his disciples for what they were going to face.

"I have told you these things, so that in me you may have peace. In this world you will have trouble. But take heart! I have overcome the world."

In John 16, we see Jesus setting the ultimate example for us as leaders. He is preparing His Disciples for the hard road that is yet to come. He tells them they will be persecuted and ultimately killed. He gives them hope in the face of what we would view as a hopeless road.

Jesus prepared the hearts by reminding them that He would send an Advocate, The Holy Spirit and that their grief would soon turn to joy. Jesus wanted them to know what they would face, that they are not alone, and in the end, they would see Him again.

As firefighters, our vision is clouded by the pain of this world, and it often becomes difficult to keep a godly perspective. So, when our hearts become troubled, pick up His word and read the encouragement that many received and modeled in the face of death and tragedy. They held the line of Hope and rejoiced in the face of adversity.

Hold the line and know that during our pain Jesus has promised: "Now is your time of grief, but I will see you again and you will rejoice, and no one will take away your joy." (John 16:22)

Notes
_____
_____
_____
_____
_____
_____
_____
_____

Riding the Seat – Day 70

By Keith Helms – Battalion Fire Chief (Retired) Charlotte Fire Department and International Board Member

"God made him who had no sin to be sin for us, so that in him we might become the righteousness of God."

II Corinthians 5:21 NIV

Consider this: I remember the first time that I "rode the seat" on an engine company. In Charlotte, riding the seat refers to the officer in charge. I was a Firefighter 1, working for a firefighter on another shift. I wasn't asked to ride the seat; I was given the order. As would be expected, we had a box alarm about 1 hour into the tour. Knowing that my company would be first in, I made certain that my external persona reflected calmness and confidence, while my internal world went spastic. I desperately wanted to do well in front of the other firefighters. I wanted to show that I had what it takes to be an effective leader, even though I had no leadership training at that point. Fortunately, it was a false alarm. I was able to stumble through the appropriate radio communications, even using all of the correct 10-codes. I wasn't proud or boastful after the call. I was overwhelmingly relieved. Thinking back on this incident, I can see that I was foolishly seeking the approval of the other firefighters, hoping that I could be perfect in my performance. While I acknowledge that we should always try to do our best, doing our work "...as unto the Lord", we can often fall into the trap of living for the approval others and perfection. This inevitably leads to a pressure-filled, performance-based style of relating. I know some officers who are so focused on being perfect on the fire scene that it affects how they supervise their crews. Instead of working to simply do a good job, they are driven to have an error free incident. Then, when the incident does not go perfectly (FYI : no structure fire goes perfectly), they look for someone to blame. They may blame themselves, or they find a firefighter to blame. Either way, someone needs to be punished. I can affirm that self-inflicted punishment can often be brutal.

Fortunately, God delivers a different message. We have no need to be obsessed with perfect performances, the approval of others, and a shame/blame style of relating. As believers, we have been given the righteousness of Christ. We are fully forgiven and fully loved by the only one that controls our eternal destiny. Who we are is based on our identity in Christ, not our performances. Step away from foolish thinking that is contrary to God's word. Seek His approval; this will give you the freedom to enjoy your work and to love as Christ loves.

Triumphal Entry – Day 71

By Wayne Detzler – International Board Member and Fire Chaplain (Retired)

The reaction of Jesus to His "triumphal entry" is very poignant. As they drew near the city of Jerusalem, Jesus wept. He lamented: ""If you had known, even you, especially in this your day, the things that make for your peace! But now they are hidden from your eyes." (Luke 19:41-2 NKJV) The crowd had missed the point completely. If only they had known—they couldn't take it in. If only they had believed—they were set in their rejection. The saddest words in our language may be, "if only." On Palm Sunday, please pray as I preach in chapel and over closed circuit TV at Elim Park. Pray that many will take this opportunity to turn to Jesus.

Notes

_____
_____
_____
_____
_____
_____
_____

Missing a Fire – Day 72

By Craig Duck – President/Missionary

Read Hebrews 10:19-25

Encouragement for the day – "Not forsaking the assembling of ourselves together, as the manner of some is; but exhorting one another: and so much the more, as ye see the day approaching."

Hebrews 10:25 KJV

The other day I missed a fire that our department was dispatched to. A neighboring town had called for assistance on a barn fire that required multiple companies to help extinguish the flames. This is not the first time in my life that I have missed a fire. This particular time I was working a fundraiser for the volunteer department I serve with. In the past, I have missed fires because our company had been dispatched on a medical local just before the box alarm was dispatched. Most firefighters hate missing fires because they truly believe they can make a positive difference on every emergency scene.

Christian firefighters are encouraged to regularly meet in a local Bible believing church. When we try and walk alone in our faith, we will inevitably stumble and fall in some way. Meeting with other Christians is an awesome privilege that helps to build steadfastness and perseverance of our faith. How else can we stir each other up to love others and to do good things for our fellow man? Sadly, many Christian first responders choose not to regularly attend a local church. These Christian first responders have all of the excuses in the world for not attending and certainly don't feel like most firefighters when they miss a fire. May all of us strive to make attending our church services a priority.

Lord, thank you for giving to me like-minded people who can help me to grow closer to you.

Encouragement is the word on the street!!

Notes

_____
_____
_____
_____
_____
_____
_____
_____

Discouraged – Day 73

By Wayne Detzler – International Board Member and Fire Chaplain (Retired)

"Why am I discouraged? Why is my heart so sad? I will put my hope in God! I will praise him again—my Savior and my God!"

Psalm 42:5, 11; 43:5 NLT

At first glance, this verse looks like a downer. It is the prescription for recovery from discouragement, or "spiritual depression" as Dr. Martyn Lloyd Jones called it. So here it is in a nutshell. First, God is the source of endless hope—the best is yet to come. Second, praise lifts us out of the doldrums—start singing a worship song or whistling one. Third, the reality is that He is our Savior and our God. This is sort of a spiritual cognitive therapy. And it is unbelievably effective. Take it from a melancholic like me!

1. How have you been discouraged lately?

2. In what ways can you actively avoid discouragement?

3. How has God blessed you recently?

Report of People Trapped – Day 74
By Craig Duck – President/Missionary

Read II Peter 2:4-11

Encouragement for the day – "Then the Lord knows how to rescue the godly from trials, and to keep the unrighteous under punishment until the day of judgment,"
II Peter 4:9 ESV

Whenever firefighters hear the words "reported people trapped" in the dispatch, they are prepared to go all out to rescue them. I have seen firefighters give 110% to rescue those who are trapped by the flames. Doors get forced open quicker; ladders are raised faster and search teams push further than normal if they think the reward is greater than the possibility of injury. We do this because we as firefighters do not want anyone to have to go through the awful death due to fire.

II Peter chapter two speaks to me of God's patience and desire that His own not suffer the consequences of sin. We read of times when people faced judgment because of their actions and how God rescued His own out of their situations. Noah is mentioned in this passage along with Sodom and Gomorrah and righteous Lot. Sometimes Christian firefighters can become trapped in their sins. It happens slowly over time, and then one day you realize that you need help. When you read through the Bible, you will learn of Godly folks who made bad decisions in life. As they cried out to God for mercy, He rescued them from their sin. God provides hope for believers; in fact, He has a plan for each and everyone who has trusted in Jesus Christ as Lord and Savior (Jeremiah 29:11). Confess your sins to God today and allow Him to rescue you out of your current state. Then and only then can you faithfully serve Him and avoid punishment.

Lord help me today to follow you wherever you lead me.

Encouraging first responders to keep the faith!!

1. What personal sin has hampered your relationship with God?

2. How can you avoid those situations that cause you to sin?

Living Loudly – Day 75

By Wayne Detzler – International Board Member and Fire Chaplain (Retired)

When the Holy Spirit is moving, life becomes exciting. One of my heroes is Wang Mingdao. In the depths of torture and imprisonment, he wrote: "[The Lord] will bring me out into the light; I will see his righteousness." (David Aikman, Jesus in Beijing, 56) After 22 years in prison, he was forced out of prison. His witness had become too dangerous for the Chinese communist authorities. Groups of believers multiplied throughout the prison. After leaving prison, he settled in Shanghai and turned his energies to encouraging the revival among the house churches. Nothing stopped him. As his biographer, Lian Xi summarized: Wang "remained an unrivaled symbol of uncompromising faith until his death [at age 91]." (Redeemed by Fire, 221) Wang's life spanned almost the entire twentieth century; his witness embraced the world. Wang lived out loud, celebrating the abundant life in Jesus.

Command Vests – Day 76

By Craig Duck – President/Missionary

Read Ephesians 4:17-24

Encouragement for the day – "and that you put on the new man which was created according to God, in true righteousness and holiness."

Ephesians 4:24 NKJV

Command vests have become popular in the fire service in recent years. More than likely brought over from the military, command vests let folks know what specific functions people are in charge of. The incident commander and the safety officer are the two most used vests that you see in the pictures circulating around social media. Our department has command vests that are carried on our first out piece of equipment. The only problem with our vests is nobody seems to wear them. The vests will never be able to fill their intended purpose until someone takes them out of the pouch and puts them on.

Paul in the book of Ephesians has just eloquently told the Ephesian people, as well as us, an important lesson. Our former lives which were characterized by all sorts of selfish sin should be "put off" and should be replaced with holiness and righteousness. This task is never easy for the first responder serving in today's fire service. The crowd always wants us to go in a direction that is in opposition to God. Paul encourages us to fully depend upon the Spirit's leading and transforming power as we moment by moment choose to obey God, putting on the new man. Don't be like those command vests in my department that never get used, choose today to put on the new man and be a good testimony for Jesus Christ so that others may know of His great love for them.

Lord, help me today to be obedient to the truths contained in the Bible.

Encouraging first responders to keep the faith!!

Notes

_____
_____
_____
_____
_____
_____
_____

The Eastern Gate – Day 77

By Wayne Detzler – International Board Member and Fire Chaplain (Retired)

The Eastern Gate of ancient Jerusalem is shut, sealed up. Ezekiel explains: "And the LORD said to me, 'This gate shall be shut; it shall not be opened, and no man shall enter by it because the LORD God of Israel has entered by it; therefore it shall be שכינה shut.'" (Ezekiel 44:1 NKJV) "According to Jewish tradition, the Shekhinah (Divine Presence) used to appear through this gate, and will appear again when the Messiah comes." ("Golden Gate," Wikipedia) It was Isaiah Martin who popularized this concept in gospel song more than a hundred years ago when he wrote:

I will meet you, I will meet you
Just inside the Eastern Gate over there;
I will meet you, I will meet you,
I will meet you in the morning over there.

Notes

_____
_____
_____

Foam Operations – Day 78
By Craig Duck – President/Missionary

Read I Peter 4:7-11

Encouragement for the day – "And above all things have fervent love for one another, for "love will cover a multitude of sins."

I Peter 4:8 NKJV

Foam operations have been around the fire service for a number of years, although foam itself has changed dramatically. My father used to tell me of protein foam that they would occasionally use which would smell awful after applying it on the fire. I remember seeing training videos of firefighters using high-expansion type foam on basement fires and shipboard fires. Aqueous film forming foam (AFFF), or "A" triple "F" foam as it was commonly referred to, began to be utilized when I first became a firefighter. Foam works because it covers the vapors that are being produced by the flammable liquid, not allowing them to ignite.

If you have served in the fire service for any length of time, you will soon discover that first responders are not perfect. Our ranks are filled with men and women who come from different backgrounds and have various expectations. Often within a department disagreements and arguments will arise due to some of these differences. "Hatred stirs up strife, But love covers all sins" (Proverbs 10:12 NKJV). The Christian first responder is encouraged to constantly show forth love to others in the station. We live in a world where it is easy for us to point out ones faults. Love, on the other hand, covers, excuses and forgives others. Love allows us to forbear, or better stated to be patient with others in our department. God tells us that when we love others as He loves, we will cover a multitude of sins.

Lord, give me courage today to see others through Your eyes and learn to love them like You do.

Encouragement, setting the standard in the fire service!!

Notes
_____
_____
_____
_____

Spiritual Milk – Day 79

By Wayne Detzler – International Board Member and Fire Chaplain (Retired)

"Like newborn babies, you must crave pure spiritual milk so that you will grow into a full experience of salvation. Cry out for this nourishment, now that you have had a taste of the Lord's kindness." (1 Peter 2:2-3 NLT) Bob Hopkins taught me these verses when he discipled me more than sixty summers ago. They have steered me through spiritual growth, and they are the core of my prayer for each of our family members each day. The beauty is this: they are as applicable for 7-year old Emma as they are for Margaret.

1. How have grown in your faith in the last year?

2. Who are you discipling so that the both of you can grow?

3. What Biblical principle has God taught you recently?

Division C – Day 80

By Craig Duck – President/Missionary

Read Isaiah 6:4-8

Encouragement for the day – "Then I heard the voice of the Lord saying: Who should I send? Who will go for Us? I said: Here I am. Send me."

                                                  Isaiah 6:8 Holman Christian Standard

      Since the advent of the incident command system (ICS) buildings have sides that are designated by letters. Typically departments will attack the vast majority of fires from side "A" or the front of the building. While some departments will routinely send companies to the "C" side of the building, most will have to locate a company to send. Once the incident commander identifies who will be operating in the rear of the building, they will designate this area as Division "C" and also identify the group leader.

      In today's Bible verse we are in a fascinating portion of the book of Isaiah. We find ourselves listening in to a conversation between the Lord and Isaiah. This section is commonly referred to as the commissioning of Isaiah. God has a job for someone to do, and without hesitation, Isaiah says "Here I am. Send Me." Can you imagine what the fire service would look like if every

Christian firefighter had that kind of attitude? God has a plan for each and every one of us. As we obediently follow Biblical principles in our life, God will provide opportunities for us to serve. Some will be needed to evangelize, others to disciple or start a Bible study in their station. When all of us choose to answer the call like Isaiah did, we will begin to see real change in the fire service and perhaps even a revival. Are you up for the challenge?

Lord thank you for using people to accomplish your will. Help me today to listen to your voice.

Encouraging first responders to keep the faith!!

1. What kind of task do you feel God has equipped you with to serve Him in the fire service?

2. What hinders you from serving God?

Hurry Up God – Day 81

By Wayne Detzler – International Board Member and Fire Chaplain (Retired)

The psalmist was on the edge when he wrote: "Quick, Lord, answer me—for I have prayed. Listen when I cry to you for help!" (Psalm 141:1 TLB) Every translation of Scripture shows this urgency. Sometimes, I just wish God would do something! Anything! But that He would do it now! Later on, we get some perspective, when the psalmist writes: " The Lord is fair in everything he does and full of kindness. He is close to all who call on him sincerely." (Psalm 145:17-18 TLB) O God, help me to wait when I want You to hurry! Amen.

1. In what ways have you been impatient with God?

2. What are some practical things you can do to slow down and listen to God?

3. How has God answered your prayers in the past?

Zero Tolerance – Day 82
By Craig Duck – President/Missionary

Read I John 3:1-10

Encouragement for the day – *"But you know that he appeared so that he might take away our sins. And in him is no sin."*

I John 3:5 NIV

When I first became a firefighter, the term "zero tolerance" was not used in the fire service. During my time as a Washington, DC firefighter is the first time I heard that phrase utilized. We had several firefighters that became caught up in the drug scene, and it affected their work habits and endangered fellow firefighters. Wanting to send the message to every firefighter that drugs would not be tolerated, management created a zero-tolerance policy. Get caught using drugs, and you would be fired, no exceptions.

God has a zero-tolerance policy when it comes to obtaining eternal life. Get caught sinning one time, and you're out. It doesn't matter the type or severity of the sin that you commit, in God's eyes any sin is enough to keep someone out of heaven. God has the right to do this because "in him, there is no sin." While that is a devastating blow to mankind because all of us have sinned (Romans 3:23), God also has made a way of escape. I John Chapter 3 is a fascinating chapter that explains just how much God loves us. He has provided a way to pay the penalty for our sins and enable us to have a right relationship with Him. Through Jesus Christ alone we can truly experience the forgiveness of our sins. Trust in Him today and begin to learn what true love is all about.

To learn more on God's plan for firefighters and how to have a personal relationship with Jesus Christ visit our website for all the details.

www.fellowshipofchristianfirefighters.org

Encouraging firefighters and first responders to keep the faith!!

Don't Quit – Day 83

By Wayne Detzler – International Board Member and Fire Chaplain (Retired)

"You keep him in perfect peace whose mind is stayed on you, because he trusts in you."

Isaiah 26:3 ESV

Very early I was shaken awake by the Lord—it must have been about 2 A.M. As I meditated on this verse, peace flooded my heart and I got up to enjoy the nighttime calm and cool. Outside it was 81 degrees. Again, the lesson became real, that God's peace surpasses all understanding. (Phil. 4:6-7) Working on a book project for one of my former students, the Lord seemed so near, so overwhelming. Later I checked my verse in The Message and found this refreshing version: "People with their minds set on you, you keep completely whole, Steady on their feet, because they keep at it and don't quit." (Jer. 26:3 The Message) As our dear Prexy Edman put it: "Never doubt in the darkness what God has shown you in the daylight." And he added: "It's always too soon to quit."

Wildland Firefighting – Day 84
Craig Duck – President/Missionary

Read Colossians 1:9-18

Encouragement for the day – *"that you may walk worthy of the Lord, fully pleasing Him, being fruitful in every good work and increasing in the knowledge of God;*
Colossians 1:10

Several times throughout my career we have been called to fight a fire in the woods. The last time involved our whole region responding to many such fires. The wind had played a major factor in these fires and departments had responded to several hundred fires in a short amount of time. The news was able to capture a lot of the fires, and my friend in California viewed our operations. I will never forget how hard he laughed seeing firefighters in structural firefighting gear wearing their SCBA's fighting brush fires. To him, they were using the wrong equipment and the wrong tactics, not having much knowledge on how to fight wildland fires.

The Bible encourages us to live our life in a way that is pleasing to God. To accomplish this task, Christian first responders must know and understand God. Knowing God can only be accomplished through our regular reading and studying the word of God. Those who chose to live their life on their own, apart from God, are just as foolish as we were trying to extinguish those wildland fires. When a firefighter has the proper tools, training, and desire to fight fires, there is nothing that they can't accomplish. Similarly, when a Christian first responder has the right tools, training, and desire, they will bear much fruit and be pleasing to God.

Lord, help me to fully understand Your perfect will for my life by daily studying the Bible.

Encouragement, pass it around!!

Notes
_____
_____
_____
_____
_____
_____
_____

Bible Heroes – Day 85

By Wayne Detzler – International Board Member and Fire Chaplain (Retired)

One of my Bible heroes is Barnabas. He invested his life in others. The following is an example, as Barnabas mentors the new believer, Saul of Tarsus AKA Paul. "Then Barnabas took him under his wing. He introduced him to the apostles and stood up for him, told them how Saul had seen and spoken to the Master on the Damascus Road and how in Damascus itself he had laid his life on the line with his bold preaching in Jesus' name. After that, he was accepted as one of them, going in and out of Jerusalem with no questions asked, uninhibited as he preached in the Master's name." (Acts 9:27-29 The Message) Paul became famous traveling the ancient world, writing almost half of the New Testament. Barnabas quietly moved on and discipled John Mark.

Notes

_____

_____

_____

_____

Coffee and the Word – Day 86

By Wayne Detzler – International Board Member and Fire Chaplain (Retired)

As he retires this week, Chaplain Glenn Havumaki gave a coffee mug to each of us on the team. It reads: "Good morning! This is God. I will be handling all of your problems today. I will not need your help. So, relax and have a great day." It brings to mind the terse verse that says: "casting all your care upon Him, for He cares for you." (1 Peter 5:7 NKJV) What a perfect way to blend two of my favorite practices: meditating on the Lord. . . And drinking coffee.

1. What type of situations make you worry?

2. How can you accomplish the task of "casting all your care upon Him?"

3. How has God delivered you from worry in the past?

Fireground Formulas – Day 87

By Craig Duck – President/Missionary

Read Luke 10:25-37

Encouragement for the day – "Love the Lord your God with all your heart, with all your soul, with all your strength, and with all your mind; and your neighbor as yourself."

Luke 10:27 Holman Christian Standard

The fire service implores the use of fireground formulas to be more efficient in fireground operations. In the District of Columbia Fire and EMS Departments pump manual, there is a whole chapter dedicated to the use of formulas. In that chapter, you will find a formula to figure out the correct engine pressure to maintain to have adequate water at the nozzle. Simply stated the formula is EP (engine pressure) = NP (nozzle pressure, which is 100 psi) + FL (friction loss) +/- Elevation. A pump operator can quickly add those numbers up in his/her head and know for sure that the crew inside is receiving the correct amount of water at the right pressure. Formulas have been designed to figure out nozzle reaction, friction loss, number of tankers needed for water supply, and many more. Think back of all the formulas you have used over the years, and you can easily come up with over a dozen. Each formula has been proven to be effective in its design and ease of use by first responders.

    The Bible talks about another formula that will help first responders to keep on track in their personal life. The formula is simple and easy to use. God's formula for success in the fire service is; God first, Family second, and others before self. As we were talking about this subject the other day one of the firefighters came up with a better way to remind us of the formula; Faith, Family, and Firefighting. These duties are designed to be worked on in the order stated. When a first responder mixes up the order his/her life will become messed up. We all know what happens when we don't use our fireground formulas correctly and not following God's plan will have the same outcome. The fire service needs to get back to having our priorities in order. Luke encourages us to love God with every ounce of energy we have and to remember others before we do anything for ourselves. This can be difficult in today's fast pace fire service, but the rewards outweigh the difficulties of not following God's formula for life.

    Lord, help me today to keep my priorities in order as I serve the community you have called me to.

Encouragement is contagious!!

God Speaks Through History – Day 88

By Wayne Detzler – International Board Member and Fire Chaplain (Retired)

As a lifelong history professor, I have marveled at the powerful demonstrations of God's hand in history. Think, for instance, of the defeat of Napoleon that opened the door for a powerful revival to sweep Europe. The psalmist employs history as a primary form of Christian apologetics:

"For I will show you lessons from our history, stories handed down to us from former generations. I will reveal these truths to you so that you can describe these glorious deeds of Jehovah to your children and tell them about the mighty miracles he did."
 Psalm 78:3-4 Living Bible

Someone said: "If we would start listening to the lessons of history, history would stop repeating itself."

Sanctification Stabilizers – Day 89

By Keith Helms – Battalion Fire Chief (Retired) Charlotte Fire Department and International Board Member

"Blessed be the God and Father of our Lord Jesus Christ, which according to his abundant mercy hath begotten us again unto a lively hope by the resurrection of Jesus Christ from the dead,"

I Peter 1:3 KJV

When a truck company is setting up its aerial ladder, it is crucial that they set the outriggers to stabilize the truck. This, along with proper spotting of the apparatus, ensures the safety of the firefighters climbing the ladder. An improperly located or set-up aerial is a catastrophe in the making. No firefighter wants to have the experience of being on a ladder when it falls due to unsafe set-up.

Stabilizing the truck is a good picture of our daily walk with Christ. God has provided spiritual stabilizers to keep us safe from falling. His desire is that we walk the narrow path of righteousness and He has provided all that we need for spiritual stability (1 Peter 1:3). Primarily, God has given us three provisions for our safety. First, He has given us the Word of God, the Bible for our instruction (Psalm 119:11, 105; 2 Timothy 3:14-4:5). Second, He has given us the Holy Spirit (John 16:5-15). All believers in

Jesus Christ are indwelt by the Holy Spirit. Third, He has given us other believers, the Church, for our encouragement and guidance (Heb. 3:13; Heb. 10:24-25). God has provided these stabilizers to keep you from falling (Jude 24); and when you do fall or stumble, He has provided the path to restoration (1 John 1:5-2:2). Check your stabilizers. Don't be a fool and think that you can live without them.

1. How has God provided for your needs this past year?

2. What Bible verses bring you comfort during difficult times?

3. In what ways can you be better prepared to remain stable during hard times?

When Leaders Pray – Day 90

By Wayne Detzler – International Board Member and Fire Chaplain (Retired)

Historically, Presidents of the United States have proclaimed days of Thanksgiving. During crises, some have also proclaimed days of prayer. But God answers only when leaders set the example of prayer. "[King] Jehoshaphat was afraid; he set himself to seek the LORD, and proclaimed a fast throughout all Judah. Judah assembled to seek help from the LORD; from all the towns of Judah they came to seek the LORD." (2 Chronicles 20:3-4 NRSV) Today we need leaders on every level of government with courage enough to pray!

1. What leadership position has God placed you in?

2. How can you better pray for those under you?

3. What are some specific prayer requests that have been placed on your heart?

Mission Statement – To glorify God in the fire service by building relationships that turn first responders heart and minds toward Christ (Philippian 2:11), equipping them to serve Him (Ephesians 4:12)

Vision Statement – To encourage one another to share the vision with the fire service through **W**itnessing, **P**raying, **T**eaching the Word, **W**alking worthy.

Contact Information
International Office
249 Rochichi Drive
Boydton, VA 23917
443-336-9859
Firequacker621@aol.com

CFHub

www.fellowshipofchristianfirefighters.org

www.ingramcontent.com/pod-product-compliance
Lightning Source LLC
Chambersburg PA
CBHW071508040426
42444CB00008B/1542